HOPE
FOR
LEADERS
UNABRIDGED

Alison,
From one leader
to another... Hope,
you enjoy! best,
all my Hope

Paperback ISBN: 978-0-9864371-3-7

Printed in the United States of America

Published by
Red Letter Publishing
San Francisco, California
www.RedLetterPublishing.com

Contents

SECTION II — PERSONAL GROWTH

SECTION III — COACHING & ORGANIZATIONAL DEVELOPMENT

SECTION IV—LESSONS FROM THE CLASSROOM

SECTION V—PEARLS FROM ENTERTAINMENT

Acknowledgements

We would like to express our heartfelt gratitude to those who helped in the completion of this book: our colleagues, partners, featured and contributing writers, professors, students, and all of the businesses with whom we have worked through the years. All contributed towards the completion of *HOPE for Leaders Unabridged.*

In particular, we would like to thank our editorial review board: Robert Johnson, Ph.D., Robin Hinkle, Ph.D., Hilke Richmer, Ed.D., and Jennifer Terry, PHR, SHRM-CP.

Special thanks to Iam Bennett whose artistic vision for our website, our newsletter, our presence at conferences, and now our first book has been incredibly important to building the brand which is HOPE, LLC.

Also, we would like to thank our writing mentor, Cathy Fyock, whose book *On Your Mark* was instrumental in helping us find an audience and voice for this book.

We would also like to thank our copy and line editors as well as our publisher from Red Letter Publishing.

Foreword

The HOPE for Leaders leadership newsletter began six years ago, when we started HOPE. From our previous lives in both large Fortune 100 companies and small consulting firms, we've regularly been writing articles and policies, first to present at conferences and develop trainings, and then to assemble other people's thoughts on leadership and training as editors. The first edition of the HOPE for Leaders newsletter came out the first month HOPE was in business and has expanded in length, content, and readership almost every month since.

When preparing content for the newsletter each month, our newsletter guidelines state that articles should be brief enough to be digested quickly; the entire newsletter should be short enough to finish in a single sitting, yet stimulating enough to trigger inspiration or discussion. It has what many newsletters do — a couple of featured articles, a few capsules, and a quote — but we intended for our readers to look forward to each month's edition, to get a quick, inspirational leadership "hit" rather than to dismiss it as one more of the same.

This ease of reading remains a priority to us, but we've seen that not everything fits within the short-and-sweet format. Sometimes, unfortunately, we'd receive good articles that were two to three times longer than we could put in the newsletter. Other times, someone would pick up the newsletter halfway through a series and might not have access to the previous articles on a topic — a different problem of length.

A year ago we were talking with several of our regular writers, and we came up with the idea for *HOPE for Leaders Unabridged*, a book where we could take some of our favorite articles and give them more "airtime," so to speak. With a book, we could allow certain series to be published in full, and therefore we could do the "deep diving" for our readers that wasn't possible with a newsletter.

Therefore, in this book, you will see some of the best topics that we've covered in the last five years, including leadership, communications, Human Resources, interpersonal interaction, and other general business topics. They are fun, quick reads, and are meant not only to educate you on a topic but to give you some actionable items and ideas that you can use in your daily life.

About the Authors

Several types of authors have contributed to the HOPE for Leaders newsletter as well as this book, *HOPE for Leaders Unabridged*. The editing and a good portion of the writing come from my husband and business partner, Dr. Joe DeSensi, and me, Dr. Hope Zoeller. We have regular contributors, whom we refer to as "featured writers" and who have written many articles over the years (generally three or more per year). We also rely on our colleagues who write the occasional article (or even just one article) on a topic near and dear to their hearts, and we refer to these as "guest writers." Having consistent voices throughout the years while constantly adding new ideas to the mix has been part of the success of growing the HOPE for Leaders newsletter readership over the last five years. I would like to take a moment to introduce readers to all of the authors who have contributed to this book:

Hope Zoeller, Ed.D.

Dr. Hope Zoeller is Founder and President of Helping Other People Excel, LLC (HOPE). HOPE specializes in leadership development for leaders at every level of an organization. For over 13 years of her professional career, Hope worked at UPS in various roles including Customer Service, Training and Development, and Employee Relations. For the past 10 years, she has been consulting with numerous organizations on leadership development. Hope is also a Professor at Webster University in the Master of Human Resource program and at Spalding University in the Master of Business Communication program. She holds a Doctorate in Leadership Education from Spalding University, a Master of Education in Training and Development from the University of Louisville, and a Bachelor of Arts in Communications and Psychology from Bellarmine University.

Hope lives in Louisville, Kentucky with her husband, Dr. Joe DeSensi. In her spare time, she enjoys international travel and yoga.

Her favorite leadership authors are John Maxwell, Stephen Covey, and Ken Blanchard. Her favorite leadership books are *Developing the Leader Within You* by John C. Maxwell, *Crucial Conversations* by Kerry Patterson, Rob McMillan, and Al Switzler, *Seven Habits of Highly Effective People* by Stephen Covey, and *Leadership and The One Minute Manager* by Ken Blanchard.

"A leader is a dealer in hope."
— Napoleon Bonaparte

Joe DeSensi, Ed.D.

Dr. Joe DeSensi is a business owner, writer, speaker, inventor, and graduate school professor. Joe has worked with clients ranging from Fortune 500 companies to federal and local government; he has started several businesses, including his educational consulting company Educational Directions, a consulting firm that works with school districts across the Southeast United States. He has helped patent several software programs in law enforcement and education, including his creation and launch of a national methamphetamine tracking product called MethCheck. Joe also teaches graduate classes in leadership, operational design, and technology at Webster University and Spalding University. Joe is a regular conference speaker in the fields of leadership, Human Resources, education, and technology.

Joe is a Louisville native and holds an undergraduate degree from Bellarmine University, a graduate degree in Computer Resource Management from Webster University, and a Doctorate in Leadership Education with a focus on managing technology from Spalding University.

Joe is a Senior Consultant for HOPE, LLC and is the coauthor of the book: *Turning Around Turnaround Schools: What to Do When Conventional Wisdom and Best Practice Aren't Enough.*

His favorite leadership authors are Margaret Wheatley, Fritjof Capra, and Scott Adams. His favorite leadership books are *Leadership and the New Science: Discovering Order in a Chaotic World* by Margaret Wheatley and *The Web of Life* by Fritjof Capra.

> *"When the best leader's work is done,*
> *the people say, 'We did it ourselves.'"*
> — *Lao Tzu*

Featured Writers

G. Tom Roach, Jr., MBA

Tom served as a military officer for over 26 years in places such as South Korea, the Caribbean, and two deployments in the Middle East. He is a senior aviator and has received over a dozen performance and achievement awards during his military career. As a civilian, he is an experienced group facilitator and Baldrige examiner, and he has worked with numerous government and non-profit organizations on strategic planning and process improvement. A leader and volunteer in religious and civic organizations, Tom is a regular speaker on leadership and management and a regular contributor for HOPE, LLC.

Tom is a Central Kentucky native and resides in Shelbyville with his wife and daughter. He completed his undergraduate degree in History and Army ROTC at the University of Kentucky in 1989. In 2010, he completed his MBA in Military Management at Touro University International. He is a doctoral candidate in the University of Charleston's Executive Leadership program. In his spare time, Tom is a certified firearms and hunter education instructor and serves on the Kentucky Fish and Wildlife Hunter Education Advisory Board.

His favorite leadership authors are King David, King Solomon, and Stephen Covey. His favorite leadership books are the Bible, *The Speed of Trust* by Stephen Covey, and *The 4 Disciplines of Execution* by Sean Covey.

> *"Where you spend your time and money*
> *are your real priorities."*
> *— Anthony W. Adams*

Jeff Powers

Jeff has been in business for over 31 years and has proven successful as both a leader and a follower. Jeff graduated from Bowling Green State University in 1984 with a B.S. in Selling and Sales Management. Upon graduating, Jeff joined Sensormatic Electronics; after several years in the selling arena, Jeff was promoted to a senior leadership role at the age of 27.

Jeff has successfully led his own consulting business and has held senior leadership roles in various technology companies. Jeff has experience with (among other technologies) electronic article surveillance, radio frequency identification, video management software platforms, restorative justice, restorative justice mobile platforms, and others.

Jeff holds four US patents and has served on various leadership boards; of note, Jeff represented Sensormatic Electronics on the MIT Auto ID board.

Jeff married his high school sweetheart, and they have four grown children. The Powers live in Plymouth, Michigan. Jeff remains very active in various charitable and community organizations as both a volunteer and a coach.

His favorite leadership author is Donald Phillips and his favorite leadership book is Phillips's *Lincoln on Leadership*.

> *"When placed in command, take charge."*
> — *Gen. Norman Schwarzkopf, Rule #13*

Frank DeSensi

Frank DeSensi is the Founder and President of Educational Directions, LLC, which consults with schools and school districts in the Southeastern and Midwestern United States. A retired educator, Frank spent 35 years in a variety of teaching and administrative positions. Frank has taught at the university, college, secondary, and middle school levels, and, separately, worked in the Jefferson County Public Schools central office as a curriculum specialist. Frank has also held both principal and assistant principal positions in public schools.

From 1993 to 1998, Frank served as a Kentucky Distinguished Educator (DE), assisting schools that had been labeled "in decline" or "in crisis" under the provisions of the Kentucky Education Reform Act. Frank helped develop the STAR training program for new DEs and served as a trainer in the Kentucky Leadership Academy. He has patented three data-management systems for schools; in 2011, he led the development of an Academic Management Organization approach as an alternative option for turnaround schools. Frank is the coauthor of the book *Turning Around Turnaround Schools: What to Do When Conventional Wisdom and Best Practice Aren't Enough.*

His favorite leadership authors are Michael Fullan and Andy Hargreaves, and his favorite leadership book is *What's Worth Fighting For?*

"Society has consistently sought to perfect 'means' with-out thought for and sometimes at the expense of 'ends.'"
— *Albert Einstein*

Guest Writers

Jeff Nally, PCC, RPCC, SPHR, SHRM-SCP

Jeff is a nationally-recognized speaker, executive coach, and author. He is the president of Nally Group Inc., a practice that brings "results with the brain in mind" to leaders and organizations.

Jeff has 23 years of experience in Human Resources, executive coaching, and leadership development. He has been an executive leader in manufacturing and healthcare corporations, including a Fortune 100 company. He is the former executive director of two not-for-profit organizations focused on health services and post-secondary education, respectively.

Jeff holds a B.A. in Psychology from Georgetown College and an M.B.A. from Georgia State University. He has earned professional certifications in both coaching and Human Resources, and Jeff volunteers his talents advancing both of these professions.

Jeff volunteers as a board member of the Ohio Valley Charter Chapter of the International Coach Federation. He is chair of the HR Advisory Committee at Metro United Way and chair-elect of the Business School Advisory Board at Spalding University. He is a past chair of Kentucky SHRM and a past president of Louisville SHRM.

Contact Jeff at Jeff@NallyGroup.com or at www.NallyGroup.com.

Jeff's favorite leadership authors are Marshall Goldsmith, David Rock, and Marcus Buckingham. His favorite leadership books are *What Got You Here Won't Get You There* by Marshall Goldsmith, *Quiet Leadership* by David Rock, and *Go Put Your Strengths to Work* by Marcus Buckingham.

"Successful people become great leaders when they learn to shift the focus from themselves to others."
— Marshall Goldsmith

Alonzo Johnson, Ph.D.

Alonzo Johnson, Ph.D., is the Managing Partner of The OASYS Group, a talent management consulting company. He has held leadership positions in the military, higher education, and in the private business sector. Alonzo has over three decades of experience in talent management and Human Resources. His expertise includes staffing and organizational development. Alonzo's vast experience in both researching and using best hiring practices in business is shared throughout his book Hiring Made Easy as PIE. His research, which investigates attracting employees with specific work behaviors to apply for a job, is published in the Journal of Management Development. He has developed training programs on employee selection for Fortune 500 companies and has taught leaders at all levels how to hire best-fit employees.

His favorite leadership author is John C. Maxwell and his favorite leadership books are *Failing Forward: Turning Mistakes into Stepping Stones for Success* by John C. Maxwell and *Leaders Open Doors, 2nd Edition: A Radically Simple Leadership Approach to Lift People, Profits, and Performance* by Bill Treasurer.

"Leaders are people who do the right thing; managers are people who do things right."
— Warren Bennis

Whitney Martin

As a measurement strategist, Whitney's passion and expertise lies in surveys and assessments. A self-professed "data nerd," Whitney has a Master's Degree in Human Resources Measurement and Evaluation and has conducted extensive research on the predictive validity of various hiring assessment strategies.

In 2003, Whitney founded ProActive Consulting, which specializes in delivering data-supported insights on job candidates, employees, teams, leaders, customers, and organizations. Using valid and reliable assessment and survey tools, the firm provides practical, actionable information to leaders that informs business decisions and has a measurable impact on the organization's bottom line.

Whitney was a highly-rated speaker at the 2014 National SHRM Conference, has been published by the Harvard Business Review, and is a contributing author of the 2015 anthology *What's Next in Human Resources*. She is a member of the American Psychological Association (APA), the Society for Industrial & Organizational Psychology (SIOP), and the International Personnel Assessment Council (IPAC). She resides in Louisville, Kentucky and can be reached via email at whitney@consultproactive.com.

Her favorite leadership authors are Thomas Friedman and Malcolm Gladwell, and her favorite leadership book is *Drive* by Daniel Pink.

> *"I often say that when you can measure what you are speaking about, and express it in numbers, you know something about it; but when you cannot express it in numbers, your knowledge is of a meagre and unsatisfactory kind; it may be the beginning of knowledge, but you have scarcely, in your thoughts, advanced to the stage of science, whatever the matter may be."*
> — *Lord Kelvin, 1883*

Susan Draus

Susan Draus is a Louisville native who currently resides in Cincinnati, Ohio. She holds a Bachelor of Arts in Philosophy, Politics and the Public from Xavier University. Susan has been a social media coordinator and marketing strategist for numerous political campaigns in Ohio, has lobbied in Washington D.C., and has met with various officials at NATO to discuss the United States' mission and role globally. In her travels abroad, Susan has studied Business and Philosophy in Israel, France, Belgium and Italy and is proficient in Italian and Spanish as well as conversational Arabic.

As a millennial in the workplace, Susan utilizes her analytical and management skills as a Product Analyst at American Modern Insurance Group, a subsidiary of Munich Re. In this company, she is an active member of the American Modern Insurance Group Women's Network and Communication Task Force and is working toward her Associate in General Insurance designation.

Her favorite leadership author is Sheryl Sandberg and her favorite leadership book is Sandberg's *Lean In: Women, Work, and the Will to Lead.*

> *"Leadership is a series of behaviors*
> *rather than a role for heroes."*
> *— Margaret Wheatley*

Introduction

HOPE is a leadership development firm. We specialize in professional development for leaders at every level of an organization. HOPE's mission is to collaborate with organizations to develop their most valuable asset—their people—by training and coaching them to reach their highest potential.

Our first task creating this book was to review five years of newsletters and find the best and most popular articles, with particular focus on the subjects that could offer more than what was possible in the newsletter. In some cases, there would be a 150-word capsule that really deserved a 1000-word chapter, or perhaps a 500-word article that could properly expand to a 2500-word chapter to more richly form the idea along with its prescriptions and remedies.

We went back to the original authors, all of whom were happy to resume work on their original ideas for this book. In some instances, authors even paired up to collaborate on an idea about which they had both written.

We've grouped the resulting chapters into five thematic sections:

SECTION 1—Leadership

SECTION 2—Personal Development

SECTION 3—Coaching and Organizational Development

SECTION 4—Lessons from the Classroom

SECTION 5—Pearls from Entertainment

How to Use This Book

This book is adaptive and can be used in a variety of ways. You can sit down and read it from beginning to end. You can flip through and find the articles that catch your eye if you need inspiration or ideas on a specific subject.

SECTION I

Leadership

The Leadership chapters are about people in leadership positions and how they can better deal with their followers. We decided to begin the book with this section since it covers many of the themes that will be unearthed in greater depth in chapters to come. In this section:

Hope begins the section by asking you if you are a servant leader or a self-serving leader in **"What Are You Serving as a Leader?"**

Tom details how leaders plan by defining the root of an issue and making processes that address and remedy a well-defined problem in **"Don't Get Stuck Crying About What You Don't Have."**

Next, Tom discusses the difference between quality of time and quantity of time and how those concepts play into leading, planning, and prioritizing goals in **"Time is Currency—Get Focused!"**

Jeff Powers discusses time as leaders conceive it and how time is wasted when leadership loses focus in **"Create Better Priorities with a New Understanding of Time."**

Finally, Tom and Joe describe how leaders fend off project scope creep and deter others from dropping needless additional work into their laps in **"How to Combat the Good Idea Fairy."**

CHAPTER 1

What Are You Serving as a Leader?

by Hope Zoeller

Take a moment and ask yourself, "What am I serving as a leader today? Am I being a servant leader or a self-serving leader?" Answer this question with brutal honesty and you will arrive at the core of your intention and motivation as a leader.

In my coaching work with leaders, I see a struggle between being a servant leader and a self-serving one. Some leaders do not perceive an immediate "return on investment" in being a servant leader; this is especially true when the organizational culture doesn't seem to value servant leadership. In such cases, leaders are rewarded for individual results, not team results; this drives them to focus only on doing their personal best, without also helping others to do their best.

According to Ken Blanchard and Phil Hodges in their book *The Servant Leader*, one of the quickest ways you can tell the difference between a servant leader and a self-serving leader is how they handle feedback. If a self-serving leader feels the feedback threatens his or her status, he or she will react poorly; one of the biggest fears that self-serving leaders have is to lose their position and status, so they spend a great deal of time and effort protecting that status. When you give them feedback, they usually respond negatively because they perceive your constructive feedback as a sign that you don't want or need their leadership anymore.

Servant leaders, on the other hand, perceive leadership as an act of service. They embrace and welcome feedback as a source of useful information on how they can provide better value as a leader.

According to Blanchard and Hodges, another way to tell a self-serving leader from a servant leader is how they approach succession planning. Self-serving leaders are addicted to power and recognition, and afraid of loss of position, so they're not likely to spend much (if any) time or effort training their successors.

Max De Pree, author of *Leadership is an Art*, declared: "The art of leadership dwells a good deal in the future, in providing for the future of the organization, in planting and growing leaders who will look to the future beyond their own." Servant leaders want to see their organization even more successful in the next generation. Servant leadership is all about making goals clear, then rolling up your sleeves and doing whatever it takes to help people successfully achieve those goals. Along the way, servant leaders must never forget that their biggest responsibility is to grow and develop people. Bottom line, your employees don't work for you—you work for them.

The skills required to be an effective servant leader can be learned. However, leaders must keep in mind that the journey is an ongoing, lifelong learning process. For this reason, those on the path to be a true servant leader must commit to continually developing themselves in the 11 characteristics of a servant leader.

According to the Robert Greenleaf Center for Servant Leadership, there are 11 important characteristics for servant leaders:

1. **Calling**—Do others believe that you are truly willing to put your own self-interest aside for the good of the group? Servant leaders have an innate desire to help others. They never do this for their own selfish gain.

2. **Listening**—Listening is one of the most critical skills of a servant leader. Do people believe that you really want to listen, or do they think you're just waiting for your turn to talk? Servant leaders encourage people to share their ideas because they are genuinely interested in hearing them.

3. **Empathy**—Do people believe you seek to truly understand what is occurring in their lives and how it impacts them? Servant leaders make a genuine effort to recognize, perceive, and directly feel the emotions, circumstances, and problems of others. Servant leaders "walk a mile" in others' shoes.

4. **Healing**—When something devastating happens in people's lives, do they come to you and share their challenges? Servant leaders have an amazing ability to help bring calm in the face of adversity.

5. **Awareness**—Do others perceive you to have a strong awareness of what is going on? Do others perceive you to have a strong awareness of your possible role in the situation? Servant leaders are always absorbing information so they can make informed decisions about people or situations.

6. **Persuasion**—Do others follow your lead because they "have to" or because they genuinely believe in you and your ability to lead them in the right direction? Servant leaders have an ability to sell their ideas by offering compelling reasons to do something. They never force or coerce.

7. **Conceptualization**—Do others feel free to share their vision of the organization with you? Servant leaders encourage others to think outside the box. They encourage creativity and innovation and foster an environment where this can occur. They value challenging the way things have always been done.

8. **Foresight**—Do others have confidence in your ability to anticipate what might happen in the future? Servant leaders are adept at identifying patterns in the environment and projecting what could possibly occur and then having a strategy to successfully respond to it. Servant leaders learn from the past and use the information in the present to respond differently in the future.

9. **Stewardship**—Do other people think you are leading the organization in a way that will make a positive difference in the world? Servant leaders seek to leave it better than they found it by preparing the organization to contribute to the greater good of society.

10. **Growth**—Do others believe that you are truly committed to helping them grow and develop? Servant leaders strive to develop people by training and coaching them to reach their highest potential. They also seek to connect people to roles that are in alignment with their strengths, desires, and passions, which helps increase their motivation and engagement.

11. **Building Community**—Do others believe that you work to build a sense of community within the organization? Servant leaders encourage others to work together. They encourage a collaborative spirit among individuals and teams.

With those characteristics in mind, ask yourself some questions about your servant leadership:

- How am I using my position of authority to obtain agreement? Do I really want the input of others, or do I really just want them to agree and validate my opinions and ideas?
- Do I truly listen to what other people are saying with their work and actions, as well as what they're not saying? Do I listen to understand, or do I just listen to respond?
- Do I seek ways to heal my personal pain and the pain of other people? Do I communicate effectively through my words and behavior? Are my words and actions aligned? Do I "walk the talk"?
- Do I take time for regular personal reflection as a way to grow? Do I seek feedback from others to ensure others' perceptions are in alignment with my own?
- Do I seek challenges for personal and professional growth? Am I continually seeking to learn and develop myself?
- Do I advocate for others even when it means I may not get what I want?

- Am I willing to put my own personal agenda aside for the betterment of others?

Becoming a servant leader requires a tremendous amount of self-awareness. It requires you to know your strengths and understand how to maximize them, and it also requires you to know your weaknesses and how to effectively minimize them. You must be willing to see your blind spots and be open to receiving feedback about them. This journey requires reflection and a constant commitment to improve yourself.

We can all be servant leaders by taking these actions. Take a moment and ask yourself: *what do I want to serve as a leader today?* Then, commit to serving it!

CHAPTER 2

Don't Get Stuck Crying About What You Don't Have

by Tom Roach

Throughout my professional life, I've heard people complain about things beyond their control. People spend time and effort complaining about the lack of resources, leader emphasis, or clear guidance necessary to "successfully" accomplish the given task. You may have heard something like this yourself, even from a superior. Grumbling is, unfortunately, a normal occurrence; however, it distracts from accomplishing the task at hand, especially when the grumbling comes from management.

Among my teaching opportunities, I volunteer-teach hunter education in Kentucky. In the survival portion, we teach people to focus on what they have rather than what they don't. The obvious difference in these two "productivity positions" is doing nothing versus doing something.

No matter the situation, you will rarely have the time, resources, or support to develop and execute the "perfect" plan. One of America's greatest military leaders of the 20th century was General George S. Patton, most notable for his various commands during World War II in North Africa, Sicily and across Western Europe. He once said, "A good plan violently executed today is better than a perfect plan tomorrow."

Here is a simple method to organize yourself and get your team to achieve the ideal state:

First, define the root problem or issue by developing a problem statement. If the boss didn't give it to you, you and your team will have to work on that. Abraham Lincoln once said, "If I had six hours to cut down a tree, I'd use the first four sharpening my axe." The point, of course, is that preparation is the key to completing the assignment, so define the problem carefully.

Ask yourself: how big is this issue? Is it confined to a single department or does it cross lines? What was the first indicator there was an issue? Is it the root issue or is it a second- or third-order effect? If it's not the root cause, keep digging; you want to cure a disease, not treat a symptom. You can start with basic questions and then either proceed to ask five "why" questions using a fishbone model or follow a flow-chart in your analysis. I will discuss each in the following sections.

Basic questions include the Who, What, When, Where, Why and How which investigators use:

1. Who was/is involved, witnessed, or otherwise has pertinent information, including experts?
2. What was the first indication there was a problem?
3. When was it discovered?
4. Where was it discovered?
5. How was it discovered? Was it direct observation during quality assurance, customer feedback, or something else entirely?
6. Why is it a problem? Does it stem from low quality, inadequate design, not meeting customer specifications, higher-than-expected costs, or safety issues?

Asking five "why" questions, or simply **Five Whys**, is not the annoying conversational technique you might imagine. Although most commonly used in the Six Sigma world, it is applicable to most daily business activities, especially those involving human factors. It is designed to remove layers of symptoms in the search for the root cause. The number of questions may vary depending on the complexity of the situation, but usually five is normal. When asking questions, the details become important, as you can see below:

1. Why did we fail to reach our monthly sales goal? *Because customers returned 60% of the items we shipped.*
2. Why did customers return 60% of the items we shipped? *Because customers stated the items did not meet their expectations.*
3. Why did the items not meet their expectations? *Because customers stated the item description was inaccurate.*
4. Why is the description inaccurate? *Because our product line is different than depicted in the catalog.*
5. Why is the product line different than depicted in the catalog? *Because our catalog is two years old.*
6. Why is our catalog two years old? *Because Marketing revises the catalog every two years.*
7. Why do they revise the catalog on a two year cycle? *Because bulk printing catalogs results in a lower per-catalog cost.*

From our example, we see that we may be saving pennies on each catalog and costing dollars in return shipping fees and untold customer satisfaction ratings.

The **Fishbone Diagram**, also known as a "Cause and Effect Diagram" or an "Ishikawa Diagram," has the problem statement at the head of the fish. Typically, there are six M "bones" added to the spine; Man, Machine, Methods, Materials, Measurements, and Mother Nature. These categories help focus your attention on potential root causes. As you work through each bone, you may discover a combination of activities that are creating the issue. As problems increase in complexity, the Fishbone also becomes more complex.

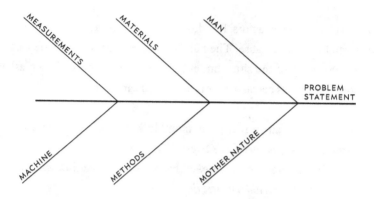

Measurements—standards, policies, laws, and regulations
Materials—input and output
Man—customers, suppliers, owners, management, and work force
Machine—equipment and technology
Methods—processes and procedures
Mother Nature—weather, geography and geology

Flowcharting or **process mapping** is a tool designed to analyze a process by breaking it into individual events, activities, or decisions that are sequentially linked. For continuity, there are standardized symbols to graphically represent each part of the process. Flowcharting is most often used in Lean to identify rework loops and non-value added (NVA) steps and may be very detailed depending on the complexity of the operation or the depth of your review.

Rework loops, also known as backtracking, are repeated steps necessary to correct defects. Documented rework loops are generally related to quality assurance processes. However, informal rework loops may exist which are not documented. For instance, my Dad's rule to live by was to "measure twice and cut once." The second "measure" is rework designed to ensure the accuracy of the cut and therefore to prevent wasting materials and time.

NVA steps are waste and, as their name suggests, add no value to the end product. Put simply: if the customer could buy processing steps independently, these are the ones they would not pay for. NVA steps are subdivided into two categories: required (R) and not required (NR). NVA-R items typically result from a legal or regulatory requirement; for example, the customer may not "want" to pay for NVA-R, but your company must comply with OSHA and EPA requirements and those costs are necessarily included in your operating overhead.

> *"If you can't describe what you are doing as a process,*
> *you don't know what you're doing."*
> — *W. Edwards Deming*

NVA-NR is the true waste. Waste may be classified into eight areas: (1) defects, (2) transportation, (3) waiting, (4) inventory, (5) motion, (6) processing, (7) personnel (under- or mis-utilization), and (8) overproduction. The latter is the most significant because it directly impacts the others.

Once your team completes the initial assessment, review it with your boss. The boss should have more experience, additional information, or at least a different perspective. At a minimum, their review can validate your work thus far in the process. If you proceed without his or her review, you may waste a lot of time going in the wrong direction. Consider this an NVA-R requirement.

Second, identify all required and available resources, including team member skills. If you and your team have undertaken a similar project, you may already have a checklist of resources; if not, start with the six M's from your Fishbone diagram for subject matter expertise. Also, with people, don't just identify someone who knows about the problem, but someone who will actually *do the work* that implements your solution. Do you need, for instance, administrative or information technology support, or will your team address those needs internally? Most likely, you will identify gaps between on-hand and required resources and skills, so be prepared to explain to your boss what you need and why you need it. You or the boss may also have to coordinate with others to fill those gaps; being accurate with this list of needs is almost as important the project itself. Asking for too little may hamper your project, while asking for too much may make the project too costly.

At a minimum, identify one person to manage knowledge (this is not the same as managing information technology). The "knowledge manager" will establish naming conventions for electronic files and folders, maintain electronic and hard copy files of the team's work, consolidate slides into a single presentation, consolidate documents into a packet for final approval, and put all the documentation into appropriate storage. As this is a pivotal position, selecting the right person is critical.

I'm reminded of the Theodore Roosevelt's expedition on the Amazon's River of Doubt. Four years after losing his bid for a third presidential term, President Roosevelt agreed to an expedition of a large tributary of the Amazon River. Unfortunately, he entrusted the expedition's organization to Reverend John Augustine Zahm, a Roman Catholic priest who taught physics at Notre Dame. Father Zahm, in turn, hired Anthony Fiala as quartermaster to plan the expedition. Unbeknownst to Father Zahm or Roosevelt, Fiala's only experience planning and leading an expedition was a failed Arctic expedition that resulted in Fiala's team being stranded on the ice for two years.

In part because of Fiala's shortcomings in planning, Father Zahm's failure to provide oversight, and Roosevelt's misplaced trust in Zahm, the expedition was troubled from the start. Once on the river, the team faced unfriendly natives, rapids, and wildlife. Disease was the greatest threat. Were it not for the experience of the expedition's leader, Colonel Cândido Rondon, all most assuredly would have perished.

Three members of the team did die. Roosevelt contracted a tropical fever that re-ignited the malaria he had contracted in Cuba. He was delirious with fever, lost over 25 percent of his body weight, and wound up battling malaria for the rest of his life, losing an estimated ten years as a result. The point is: be careful whom you entrust with the responsibility for essential information!

Third, recognize that time is your most limited and therefore most precious resource. What is your deadline? Given a fixed amount of time, identify intermediate milestones so you complete the project in the allotted time. Is this project your sole focus or do you have another "day job" competing for your time? Where are the friction points, internal checks, or in-progress reviews with the boss? For nearly any project, expect it to take 50 percent longer than your initial estimate to account for those unknown unknown elements. Whether you use a Gantt Chart, a spreadsheet, or a software program, have a systematic method to manage your available time. A good plan on time is better than a great plan late. Your team can't work 24 hours a day, seven days a week. For long projects, plan time off for the team each week. If you don't, you run the risk of losing them to burnout, fractured families that distract, or leaving the team outright.

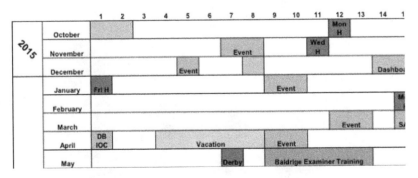

If you have a presentation requirement, make sure you have an idea of what the boss wants and how they want to see it. Establish a format and provide it to all the team members so you don't waste time you may not have. This will streamline consolidation by the knowledge manager. Rehearse every presentation, even if it's a re-hash of one you've already done; you may spot an issue previously overlooked.

Fourth, give specific tasks to individuals, or to a team under the direction of a single individual, to maintain accountability. Track progress so everyone sees it. If you have subordinate teams, give them time to meet and work without you. See the example of a task tracking chart below:

Task	Reference	Owner	Specified	Implied	Essential

Remember Theodore Roosevelt's saying "Do what you can, with what you have, where you are." Follow this simple methodology and don't get stuck crying about what you don't have.

CHAPTER 3

Time is Currency–Get Focused!

by Jeff Powers

In the mid-1990s, a good friend and I started a media company in Dallas, Texas. My partner and I had come from completely different business backgrounds, both relatively successful in our previous endeavors, but none of what we had done before had direct correlation to what we were about to embark upon.

Our company was the expansion of my partner's idea, whereby we would re-cruit and train current and former professional athletes to report on their own sports. Hearing about football from a current player (trained by our company) made all the sense in the world, considering that most (if not all) of the com-mentary on sports at that time was being provided by professional, trained, and educated sports broadcasters. There were various "color commentators" who provided an insider's view of games, but the actual reporting was always done by broadcasters.

Who better to discuss the difficulty and pain associated with fall football camp and two-a-days then men who had gone through it? Who better to talk about the toll a 160-game schedule took on the human body than an MLB player who had played and was playing currently? They could provide opinions that broadcasters could only speculate about.

We had the opportunity to partner with Hillwood Development, which at the time was a billion-dollar firm. The founder and leader of Hillwood was Ross Perot, Jr. Ross Perot Sr.—the former IBM executive, founder of EDS, billionaire, and former candidate for President of the United States—had an office in the same building that Hillwood Development did. He heard about this potential business partner to Hillwood Development and decided to drop in on our first presentation. He arrived early and was polite and professional. He asked us if we were doing all right and if there was anything he could get for us.

In this meeting to describe our business concept and solicit funding from Hillwood, we outlined all of the goals that we were going to accomplish. We envisioned pro players reporting on every sport, in every league. Part of our plan was to recruit, hire, and train these pro players ourselves, so a big part of our foundation would be dedicated to "selling" to these pro players that our company would be a starting point for their next careers as broadcasters, and not merely as color commentators.

We prepared well for the introductory meeting with Hillwood Development. We outlined "every conceivable" option for our company. We showed all of the great things we were going to do with their financial investment in my partner and me. We had separated each of these opportunities into individual strategic plans. We had the NFL, MLB, NHL, NBA, and MLS, and we had off-shoot programming on several ideas we trademarked—"in the dugout," "in the huddle," "on the hardwood," "coaches' corner," and "on the ice." Each of these opportunities would fit into our overarching plan of having pro players reporting on every sport, every game, every day.

Here's the problem: we were underestimating the amount of work this part of the plan would require. We were going to go after current players making millions of dollars and flying high in the midst of their careers. The recruitment and education of the "right" players would take up much of our time and energy. Not to mention, each sport's network was, essentially, a business idea in its own right.

Hillwood Development took a look at all of our documentation we prepared and laid out on the board room table. Ross Perot Sr. scanned the individual and somewhat connected strategic business elements. He took his time, circled the board room, and took in what we planned. Then, he made the comment: "This looks like death by opportunity."

The message was clear: *get focused!*

In the several minutes he perused our presentation, he gathered quickly that we tried to be all things to all people. We bit off more than we—or any two guys—could ever chew. He gave us the best advice we would receive from Hillwood, along with their investment: get focused!

Think of your time as a currency—which it is—and then decide: where do I plan to spend my currency? There is only so much time in a day. We should control what we can control, and one thing we cannot control is how much time there is in a day. What we can and must control is what we do with that time, our currency. In particular, in a small startup company, setting a plan and then executing that plan is not only smart, it is imperative to the survival and longevity of the business. If you try to do too many things all at once, you will suffer the old adage "jack of all trades and master of none," which in business terms means you will have spent valuable currency on something you cannot get back and cannot undo.

We got focused, Hillwood invested in our business, and we built an impressive list of accomplishments one at a time! When it made good sense, we expanded from our core disciplines.

Focus means every ounce of your energy must be directed toward a tangible win, and once accomplished you broaden and expand. Trying to be all things to all people will lead to fragmentation and failure.

CHAPTER 4

Create Better Priorities With a New Understanding of Time

by Tom Roach

I was talking to a young man recently when he raised the idea of buying his first home. We agreed that was a great goal, and that it should be high on his priority list. I asked him about his other goals, and he quickly rattled off three or four more items that he considered his priorities. Then I asked him where he spent most of his money and his free time, and, just as quickly, he rattled off three or four different items. What struck me was not only that the two lists had nothing in common, but they were actually in conflict with one another. He was thoroughly amazed when I pointed out that his second list was his real list of priorities. He hadn't yet understood that, as Mahatma Gandhi said, "Action expresses priorities."

Chronos and *Kairos*: Differentiating the Aspects of Time

We all have limited resources. *Chronos* is the Greek word that refers to quantity of time. *Kairos* is the Greek word that refers to quality of time. We're only getting 24 hours in a day and seven days in a week, so our *chronos* is set. How much quality we get out of that time is up to us; it's a matter of effectiveness (adequacy to accomplish our purpose) and efficiency (competency with the least waste of time and effort).

As I see it, we have three options:

1. First, we can **use time**. These are the necessary evils in our lives like our daily commute to work. In Lean terminology, we may classify these as business non-value added requirements.
2. Second, we can **waste time**. Too much TV, surfing the internet or an ill-considered hobby would fall here. Again, in Lean terminology, we may classify these as non-value added, things for which no customer would be willing to pay. I believe even our hobbies should support our goals and priorities.
3. The third (and I would say best) option is to **invest time**. As with any financial investment, we should expect a return. I include time with family, serving others, bettering my community, and earning my paycheck in this category.

These are the value-added steps in our process. Since I'm investing my time, my most limited and finite resource, to earn money, it must follow that I consider those three same options (using, wasting, and investing) for financial expenditures as well. Therefore, we see that it becomes all the more important to apply our limited resources to the things that matter the most to us.

What I say about hobbies may seem a bit confusing, so allow me to explain. Having already established a common understanding of time, effectiveness, and efficiency, let's now consider levels of performance as a measure of effectiveness and efficiency. We first seek to gain *competence*—that is, the basic ability to do something successfully. Next, we seek *proficiency* or *expertise* in the particular area. Lastly, we seek *mastery*, the comprehension of true knowledge or skill. Depending on the task, it may take you multiple iterations to learn the basics for a given task. Given the limited amount of time and money we have, we reduce the likelihood we will reach mastery as we split those resources.

For example: nearly everyone plays golf, knows someone who plays golf, or at least understands the basics of golf. Does knowing the basics, or possessing basic skills, ready you to compete in the PGA?

Take Tiger Woods, who is without question one of the greatest golfers in the modern era. He didn't just show up ready to compete; he committed his whole life to perfecting his game. Two months before his third birthday, he putted with Bob Hope on the Mike Douglas Show. He reportedly broke 70 (two under par on a typical eighteen-hole round) before his thirteenth birthday. Tiger typically invests two hours before breakfast to physical fitness, and another 30 minutes before dinner. He invests two hours on the driving range perfecting his swing and 30 minutes practicing putting before lunch. The afternoon is consumed by the golf course, working on his swing and short game, and another nine holes. That, folks, is commitment to mastery—on a single skill, no less!

> *"A dream doesn't become reality through magic;*
> *it takes sweat, determination and hard work."*
> *— Colin Powell*

The point is this: because your time is precious, enjoy hobbies that are aligned with your goals and priorities and, at a minimum, avoid any hobbies that actually conflict with your goals and priorities.

Goals and Priorities

Setting priorities means focusing your effort on those items most important to achieving your overall goal. The more you narrow your focus, the more resources you can apply. As you spread resources among more and more goals, you decrease the likelihood of achieving them with excellence. Stick with two or three goals and you will likely achieve all of them; have four to ten and you may reach one or two,; have more than 11 and you will likely achieve none of them (*Four Disciplines of Execution*, 2012). Whether personally or organizationally, you can be good in a lot of areas, but you can only be *great* in a few.

Organizationally, it is imperative to carefully consider your goals and priorities. What if you're not in a position to affect the implementation of goals and priorities? No problem! Don't worry about what you can't control; worry about what you *can* control. Whether your organization has its priorities straight may be completely beyond your control. Whether you are responsible only for yourself, for 500 others, or for some number in the middle, you can affect your span of control.

First, ask yourself: "What does my customer want?" This is especially important if you are self-employed or in a leadership position with a larger company. If you don't produce what they want, you won't be in business long.

Next: "Can I make money producing what they want?" Is it in line with your current business model, or will you have to change your plan? Is this an emerging market or existing market? If existing, is it saturated? Are you filling a niche market or a wider market?

Consider, as an example, the product offerings of IBM from 1924 to the present day. It has moved from punch card production and reading equipment to electric typewriters to commercial (and then home) computers, then to business intelligence, continuity security, and green solutions. Throughout its existence, IBM generated tremendous leaps in business technology, including introduction of the industry standard personal computer in 1981. But in 2005, it sold all of its personal computer business to Lenovo. Still, IBM has consistently high rankings as a company: #12 in Brand Finance (2015 Brand Finance Global 500), #9 in Official Top Business Super-Brands (2015, The Centre for Brand Analysis), #25 in World's Most Admired Companies (2015, Fortune), #4 of Best Companies for Leadership (2014, HayGroup), #4 in Best Global Brands (2014, Interbrand), and top annual patent recipient for 20 consecutive years.

By contrast, consider Eastman Kodak. It dominated the photographic film industry for most of the 20th century and in 1976 owned a 90-percent share of the U.S. market ("The End of our Kodak Moment," *London Telegraph*, January 2012). They developed the digital camera in 1975, but dropped it for fear it would threaten their film business ("Kodak's Last Days," *NewStraitsTimes*, February, 2012). In 1997, stock prices were $93 per share; the price per share dropped to 36 cents after they filed for Chapter 11 bankruptcy protections in 2012 ("Eastman Kodak Files for Bankruptcy," *New York Times*, January 2012). Thus ended "the Kodak Moment."

Now ask, "What does the boss want?" There will likely be two parts to the answer: one quantifying (how much) and one qualifying (how good). You may have had a discussion with the boss about his expectations when you joined the team. You may also have regular performance reviews. Both of these should shape your answer. The more specific your answer, the better able you will be to meet expectations.

Generally, this is where the discussion would end, but not today. Let's delve into the "home" part of your life. Whether you are married or not, it's time to establish a plan for that other part of your life.

Try this:
- Take a piece of paper and draw a line down the middle of it.
- On the left half, write down your priorities.
- On the right half write down where you spend your free (non-work) time and your money.

Do the expenditures match what you say are your goals and priorities?

Unfortunately, few Americans have a budget (32% according to a 2013 Gallup poll), and if any plan further, it's probably limited to other financial matters like retirement accounts, a will, or property. The likelihood of having a plan that goes beyond financial aspects is remote. Sit down with your immediate family (spouse and children) and jointly develop answers to each of these questions:

1. What is our mission? That is, what is our important goal or purpose in which we have strong conviction, or our task or duty, whether assigned or self-imposed?
2. What is our family goal or vision (achievement, destination, or desired and ideal state)?
3. What are our values (what we respect, esteem highly, or consider important)?
4. What is our philosophy (our guidance in practical matters, our system of thought)?
5. What are our plans (method of acting, doing, or proceeding with purpose)?
6. Are we on the right course (path in a particular direction to progress from one point to the next)?

Why is it important to answer these questions jointly? If it's your plan, they don't all own it, in part or in whole, and are not vested in its success. Notwithstanding the soundness of your logic or the reasonableness of your conclusion, your spouse and children may not actively support it and may even actively work toward its failure. I have a friend that made such a plan and presented it to his wife; his logic was sound and took into consideration the totality of their circumstances, and the conclusion was reasonable and thoughtful. Although there were other issues in play, this methodology contributed to his divorce! The lack of collaborative planning demonstrated a lack of mutual respect. While this is, of course, an extreme outcome, I firmly believe that agreeing to answers with the questions listed above, especially before marriage, will result in a common framework for the family. With that common framework, you answer difficult questions before there is emotion or urgency attached to them.

"When dealing with people, remember you are not dealing with creatures of logic, but with creatures of emotion, creatures bristling with prejudice and motivated by pride and vanity."

— *Dale Carnegie,* **How to Win Friends and Influence People**

Through the Looking Glass

Alice and the Cheshire Cat from *Alice in Wonderland*:

Alice: Would you tell me, please, which way I ought to go from here?
The Cat: That depends a good deal on where you want to get to.
Alice: I don't much care where—
The Cat: Then it doesn't matter which way you go.
Alice: —so long as I get *somewhere* . . .
The Cat: Oh, you're sure to do that, if you only walk long enough.

What we are talking about is linking all your activities to your goals and priorities. In the military, for instance, we spend a vast amount of time developing plans to accomplish "the mission." Some leaders or teams are so attached to the plan that, when confronted with the enemy, they fight the plan and not the enemy.

Field Marshal Helmuth Carl Bernard von Moltke once said, "No battle plan survives the first encounter with the enemy." He believed orders should not be detailed, but instead provide general guidelines within which subordinates could operate. Today, the Army refers to this as *the commander's intent*. On a similar note, General Dwight D. Eisenhower once said that "plans are worthless, but planning is everything."

Tying these two thoughts together, we can see the importance of developing plans and engaging with others, at home or at work, to get their perspective so we can carefully see the fullness of the situation. We then develop flexibility within our plans to meet the changing environment and still accomplish our overall goal. If they aren't directly linked, then you're probably making great time driving on the wrong road—just moving about, turning without rhyme or reason.

CHAPTER 5

How to Combat the Good Idea Fairy

by Joe DeSensi and Tom Roach

Have you ever had a plan or a project almost finished when someone important dropped in to give his or her two cents? Meetings were already held to get others' input, plans have already been proposed and drafted and circulated, and the chosen plan was already solid and ready for action. Yet now everything is up in the air, the plan seems to be unraveling, and the scope of work is creeping. This is the legendary Good Idea Fairy that appears, injects new ideas that affect the scope, timeline, or approach, and then disappears—leaving a leader or other project manager to clean up the aftermath.

The Good Idea Fairy is not always a bad thing. Early in a process, when a group is brainstorming and gathering fresh ideas and looking at raw data, Good Idea Fairies might help combat groupthink or spark inspiration that offers alternatives that had not been submitted. With that in mind, there is a narrow window for the Good Idea Fairy being useful: at the beginning of an initiative or project. As plans solidify and planning becomes working, the Good Idea Fairy's positive contributions become fewer and fewer, and the confusion and potential rework it can instigate increases over time.

When kicking off a new initiative, the five phases of planning or project management are: initiation, planning, executing and monitoring (which run concurrently), and project conclusion. Even in less formal settings, this is the normal process one follows in getting an assignment completed. Good Idea

Fairies can play positive or neutral roles in the initiation phase and early in the planning phase.

Good Idea Fairies can also have positive input in the project closing—which might be a surprise, but when a group is deconstructing what went right and what went wrong at the end of a project, to "learn more for next time," some fresh ideas about how things could have been different can be useful. In summary, Good Idea Fairies are good for thinking phases and bad for when real work needs to be completed.

In the planning phase of good project management:
- The scope is agreed upon,
- the goals and measures of success are established,
- assumptions and contingencies are documented,
- priorities and timelines are established,
- resources are assigned,
- checkpoints are set, and
- everything is played backward from the end before the execution and monitoring begin.

This complexity of interwoven planning pieces is exactly why a Good Idea Fairy can be so dangerous. When executing a project plan, one might not remember every dependency, assumption, risk, and deliverable line item that went into each decision. To some degree, the plan has to be trusted, including that its checkpoints and monitoring will keep things on track.

This is when the Good Idea Fairy can be dangerous. To suddenly raise ideas about changing key processes or events (especially ones that fall on the critical path) can be very dangerous. Anything changing in the execution of an initiative without first consulting the project charter, assumptions, risk management plan, and project deliverables can mean death for a timeline or a budget. This is true in non-project management settings as well—there is a time for brain-storming and a time for doing, and they're separate by design.

This does not mean to be closed off to new ideas, or to not optimize. But remember that the Good Idea Fairy's suggestions often come from a less helpful, less benign place. Here are some characteristics to identifying a destructive Good Idea Fairy, just in case they are not wearing their wings or holding their Bad Idea Scepter:

- **Regularity**—They drop bad ideas or derail processes or projects all the time. Good Idea Fairy sightings are less like hunting Bigfoot and more like trying to find a TV show involving Kardashians. You don't always need to look for them; they seem to always be around, and the quality of their content is always about the same.
- **Bad Ideas**—If a person drops in and drops ideas regularly, but they are good ideas coming from a strong understanding of an issue or a depth of experience, this is not a Good Idea Fairy per se. The idea might be gruff, or the person just might not be your favorite, but if the information is helpful, you should be open to it. Conversely, Good Idea Fairies can be fun, gregarious people and might even be your friends, but their timing and ideas can hurt more than help.
- **Rookie Mistakes**—A lot of the bad ideas that come from Good Idea Fairies occur because they don't know enough of the context or subject matter well. The problem is that if Good Idea Fairy dust is sprinkled in front of leaders that also share the same lack of nuanced understanding about the subject, you might spend a lot of time suddenly having to prove the approach you had chosen to take and the decisions you have made, or, even worse, having to decide how to change things.
- **Idea Grenades**—When a Good Idea Fairy drops an idea, it rarely includes substantial time or resources invested on their part. They swoop in, drop a grenade that gobbles time or focus, and then magically disappear as quickly as they came. If such people have no accountability and

there is no cost to their budget or priorities, sometimes their ideas are less well-conceived than something they would enact on a project or process they own.

Good Idea Fairies can affect timelines, quality of output, stakeholder management, morale of the team, and the resources required to complete a task or project. Here are ways to combat or preemptively mitigate the possible effects of Good Idea Fairies:

Publish a timeline. Covey says that a goal isn't a goal until you write it down. A published timeline makes the dates and times appear more set, especially if they have been approved from higher levels of management.

Get sign-off from above. Not just on your timeline, but also on your approach, resources, and ultimately the project's goal. An idea that has sign-off from above also has air cover from above.

Charter the plan or project. By developing a vision for what you want to complete, a mission for how you are going to get there, and some metrics of success, you can either show how something does or doesn't fit inside what you are trying to accomplish. Also, the more complete and well-documented a plan, the less likely someone will throw in random ideas.

Define your scope. The charter can help draw boundaries around a project for an idea. Defining one's scope not only helps figure out what is to be accomplished, but more importantly, it is there to protect from "scope creep," or the idea that, after plans are made and resources are procured, the amount to be achieved during the current mission gradually increases (usually without an increase in resources or compensation).

Document your facts and assumptions. Facts are known truths, whereas assumptions are assertions accepted as truth. We gather pertinent facts, but we also make assumptions early in a project planning process. It is good to define those assumptions for two reasons:

1. If there are questions about why decisions were made, it is good to have documented the rationale. There could be good reasons behind things that turn out to be wrong decisions, so it is important to document the "why" behind some foundational elements to a project plan.

2. Assumptions should be revisited throughout the project. For instance, there could be some pending legislation that would mitigate a project plan. As another in-house example, the availability of certain resources will likely be based on the progress of other projects or departments in the company. We don't live in a static world; things are always changing. We need to keep apprised of anything we have learned after our planning that might affect how we execute that plan. Ultimately assumptions are confirmed (thus becoming facts), are discarded as they become irrelevant, or are proven wrong and require planning revisions.

Seek input during the planning phase. If some people are constantly adopting the Good Idea Fairy approach, begin to seek them out earlier in the process. Even if you don't incorporate their ideas, you can detail why in your scope and assumptions.

Formalize the presentation of your plan. If you plan using a white board, it might seem more "changeable" to Good Idea Fairies than if you used large paper, such as butcher paper. Paper is more permanent, it remains available for regular review, and it can prevent you covering the same ground repeatedly. Finally, on a separate note, use a professional PowerPoint slide deck to show where you are in the timeline and to define the scope.

Say yes to anything you can, short of changing anything of substance. If someone has an idea that you have already integrated into a plan, go ahead and let them have credit for it. Sometimes sharing the credit on the origins of some ideas allows you to say no to some other ideas. When getting more people involved, they become vested in its ultimate success.

Lastly, be open to the fact that Good Idea Fairies could *sometimes* have ideas worth considering. In the South, we say even the blind squirrel occasionally finds a nut. Make sure that you reject the Good Idea Fairy's suggestion on its (lack of) merit, rather than the fact that it comes from a source yet to contribute a helpful suggestion.

Solid planning, formalizing processes, and good tactical communication skills help mitigate the effects of a Good Idea Fairy when one decides to pay you a visit. No more needless scope creep or having to reopen the planning phase of something otherwise ready for work!

SECTION II

Personal Growth

For leaders, developing oneself is as important as learning how to develop others. This section focuses on skills that make people better people, no matter their position. In this section:

Joe applies project management best practices to self-management, and to the specific example of defining, tracking, and successfully completing New Year's resolutions in **"Chartering a Happy New Year."**

Jeff Powers discusses grace under fire and keeping one's principles intact during crises in **"Never Panic. Well..."**

Jeff Powers also tells a personal story about Sam Walton as a model for embracing innovation in **"Don't Fear Change!"**

Joe uses a three-part piece to explore "lag time" for noticing people that are undergoing positive changes, and how to better market those changes, in **"Reality of Personal Change versus the Perception of Change."**

Tom takes an introspective look at careers and how to maximize a person's potential in **"Do What Your Career Can Stand."**

CHAPTER 6

Chartering a Happy New Year

by Joe DeSensi

In both my Leadership Development and Operational Design graduate school classes, I teach some form of chartering and strategic goal setting. I wondered what would happen if a year were viewed as a strategic project, and New Year's resolutions thereby were SMART (Specific, Measureable, Attainable, Results-focused, and Time-Sensitive) goals. Good project management skills help sports teams, social clubs, educational groups, family projects and vacations, and multi-million-dollar business initiatives—why couldn't they help us keep our New Year's resolutions for once?

The process of chartering does not start with defining goals. Before we can set goals, we need to know what success looks like. Before we can measure success, we need to define the thing at which we are trying to be successful.

To charter a new year, one must first have a vision, an ambitious view of the year that (A) one can believe in and (B) should be something not readily attainable that offers a future brighter than the existing view of upcoming year. "Being happy" might be a vision that most people would like, but for the purposes of strategic design, let's be more specific. How about: "The new year will be a year of health, positive growth and happiness."

Now we need a Mission Statement—a statement that defines how one will attempt to realize one's vision. A mission statement is needed for us to enact the vision and distinguish this year from others. Mission statements define core purpose and core values, provide direction and focus for one's vision, form the basis for one's strategies and goals, and serve as the proverbial North Star for judging whether an activity or decision fits in one's vision for the year. An example would be something like: *In the new year, I will focus on healthy living for mind, body, and soul, and ridding myself of negative and toxic activities and people.*

Some key features:
- "I" makes it personal
- "Mind, body and soul" provides a holistic approach to oneself
- "Ridding negative and toxic" means that the vision is as much about releasing the bad as it is promoting or pursuing the good

The last part of our strategic design of the New Year's charter is to create SMART goals for the year. "Eating healthier," for instance, is a good thing to do, but it is not a strategic goal—yet.

Goals should be SMART:
- *Specific:* "I will find a nutritionist by the end of January to help me change my eating habits."
- *Measurable:* "I will read one chapter a week of the inspirational book I was given by a good friend that has sat on my shelf since my birthday."
- *Achievable:* "I will go to the doctor to make sure I am in good health and to help me decide what I should work on for the year, such as losing weight or lowering my cholesterol."
- *Results-Focused:* "I will volunteer once a month to help those not as fortunate as I am."
- *Time-Specific:* "I will say no at least once a month to a toxic friend or a negative activity that I know is bad for me."

Having both the "A" and the "T" are critical. If goals are not Achievable, they can seem overwhelming and become easily abandoned. If there is no time frame, then they will be forgotten a few months into the year (this is also why it is good to have at least a few deadlines in January—to keep the charter fresh in one's mind).

Let's add another layer of efficacy and efficiency to our New Year chartering and goal-setting process:

1. **Chunking**—Rather than only setting goals for the whole year, let's set some umbrella goals for the year but break them into monthly chunks. Chunking is a great way to show some immediate progress leading to a bigger goal without that goal feeling overwhelming and unreachable. After one gets a major SMART goal set for the year, one should set up January, February, March, and overall Q1 chunks of that goal that are also Specific, Measurable, Achievable, Results-Based, and Time Specific.

2. **Easy Wins**—There is an old saying that success breeds success. Whether it's going on a diet and losing some pounds the first week, or taking a class and acing the first test, chalking up some easy wins early can set the stage for long-term success. Make sure the January SMART goals are "gimmes" and easy to attain.

3. **Make it a "big rock"**—Most people have seen Stephen Covey's time management visual metaphor where he shows that the only way to get the big rocks, the little rocks, and the sand into the single container is to make sure one places the big rocks first. Block time out on your calendar to work on your monthly chunks of your yearly smart goals. If you try to fit it in when you have time, other things will always get scheduled over it. Make it like that department meeting or that social event that gets on your calendar early—and around which everything else has to work.

4. **Track it**—At the end of each month and quarter, review the charter for the year, the goals for the year, how you did on the previous month, and what you are going to knock out in the upcoming month. Do this four or five days before the end of the month so that you have time to clean up any SMART goals for the current month that you still have a shot of

completing, and also so you know exactly what you will be completing in the coming month. Chunking and tracking used in tandem will greatly help keep you on course for your year's goals.

You will be amazed at how easily major milestones will come to pass when properly chartered, chunked, tracked, and prioritized. The good news is that most of us already use some of these skills and techniques elsewhere in our lives, so it isn't taking on a whole new learning curve, but rather applying something known to a different part of our lives. If you have never done anything like this before and this is all new, what better way to break in this new skill set than on your own life and happiness?

Also, if you learn the skills here, you can apply them to other facets of your life very quickly. These skills are good business techniques or good project management skills; they are skills we can use in almost every aspect of our lives. Having a clear vision of what success looks like, defining the mission that will get us there, and then breaking out focused, individual deliverables is a great approach for doing, well, anything worth doing.

My last tip for chartering the New Year is to **share it**. Tell a few positive, supportive friends what you are doing. Ask them to check on you and your progress from time to time. Telling someone else adds a layer of external accountability to help you meet your SMART goals, achieve your mission, and realize your vision for the New Year.

Happy Strategic New Year, everyone!

CHAPTER 7

Never Panic. Well...

by Jeff Powers

There are many versions of the cliché "never panic"—*don't let them see you sweat* and so on. That goal is admirable; achieving that goal, and thus truly never panicking, is difficult. After all, panic is the opposite of what leaders must provide to their people.

We should always try to attain our lofty goals, but we have to be prepared for problems. We cannot be afraid of failure, or trying and then getting up after we fall. Failing one time provides an opportunity for correction, a pivot point, a learning experience.

Years ago, my family adopted an older dog from a shelter. We simply called her "Big" because, well, that's what she was. We didn't know her history or how old she was or where she had come from. We just knew, from the day we adopted her, that she would be a part of our family until her race was run. The day we brought her home (to our home that had had dogs in the past), we welcomed her a hundred percent. She did a lap or two around the house with her nose on overdrive. She oriented herself quickly and effectively to our home, now her home as well.

Our previous dogs, Labradors, were so well-behaved and such homebodies that we never worried about them leaving our property. In fact, I was impressed when they wandered 100 feet from our back door. Our property has everything a dog would want: trees, grass, and open spaces.

I had to join a conference call in my home office, so I asked my 14-year-old daughter to keep an eye on Big. She had been on point with our other dogs for years and always made sure they were where they needed to be. I had no reason to think that would change with Big. However, there were a couple change-elements that I had not accounted for: smart phones and her teenage years!

I was on the phone for about 45 minutes. I came out of my office, and my daughter was sitting at the kitchen counter texting on her phone. I asked her where Big was. She started to say, "I let her out to do her business. . ." and I immediately panicked. I couldn't believe she just opened the door, as we had done for 13 years with our other hounds, and let Big go . . . even though this was the way "we had always done things." The new model was different, but I had not explained or set expectations for her. I made the classic mistake of "assuming."

By the way, this happened in Michigan in December. Two feet of snow covered the ground. Tracking Big would not be difficult, or so I thought; her tracks were heading toward the last home she had had, some 20 miles away. I lost her tracks in the woods, came home, walked into our kitchen, and completely unraveled. My calm, professional, coaching self began ranting and raving and blaming my daughter for being careless, and I laid Big's escape right at her 14-year-old feet. This was behavior she had never seen from me. I was in violation of one of the most important leadership traits: consistency! My daughter and my family as a whole had virtually no experience with this "panic mode." I was running around with my hair on fire!

I can honestly say I learned more about myself, about practicing what we preach, and about how NOT to react in a crisis than I had ever thought possible. We have all worked with (and for) people who are volatile, inconsistent, and difficult. I always tried to never be that coworker or leader. To me, being consistent was paramount to being able to trust my people because consistency was how they knew the expectations and the parameters for their success.

I have apologized to my daughter several hundred times, and, as a 22-year-old adult, she simply says, "I hope you learned something from this." Yes, Leah, I did learn something—quite something.

In the end, we found Big a mile or so away from our home, unharmed. She lived out her last three years without venturing beyond our back yard.

I learned that it is easy to talk about things in the bright light of day. It is easy to decide how you are going to react in a crisis, but it is poor planning to be completely unprepared for bad things that will happen. I learned that when a crisis occurs (and they will), we need to do four things, the things I wish I had done the day of Big's great escape:

1. Don't panic.
2. Gather as much information as possible as quickly as possible.
3. Take charge of the situation by making a plan of action.
4. Implement your plan!

Never panic. Never assign blame. Never turn on a teammate. Never let the crisis lead you. My daughter has forgiven me for my panic and Big led a wonderful, comfortable life with us until she passed away in April 2013.

Here are the main lessons from this I would like to impart:
- Leaders must remain consistent.
- Leaders must set expectations.
- Leaders must communicate specific details to their people.
- Leaders can never panic!
- Leaders are most valuable when a crisis occurs—and sometimes the leader that emerges is not the leader of record prior to the crisis.

CHAPTER 8

Don't Fear Change!

by Jeff Powers

Many years ago, I had the opportunity to hear Sam Walton speak. Mr. Sam (as he was commonly called) was still Chairman of Walmart at the time. He talked about one of the only constants in business and life: change. His advice to the audience was to become very comfortable with change. "A person, in order to be successful, has to embrace change," Mr. Sam said.

At the heart of change is trying something new. The ability for a leader to risk failure by trying something new is extremely important. It seemed to me what Mr. Sam was trying to communicate was that, in life and in business, change will happen. For things to evolve, change must happen. You can either sit back and wait and hope that the change is in your favor, or you can be an agent of the change and control the change (as much as you can).

Shortly after hearing Mr. Sam speak, I had the opportunity to meet with him at Walmart. I presented an opportunity for Walmart to implement a technology they had not previously considered applicable for them or their customers. The technology, a loss prevention technology that helped deter shoplifters, was relatively new and there were no other mass retailers like Walmart using the technology. The other retailers that had adopted this new technology had such different businesses that it was not possible to compare a Walmart operation to, say, a department store. Executive leadership was very much against trying this new technology for fear that it would alienate and upset their core customers.

The technology consisted of an RF antenna at the exit and small, well-placed "tags" on high-value merchandise. When one of the "tags" entered the exit antenna field, it sounded an alarm. The system couldn't tell whether someone was trying to steal, or a Walmart associate had simply forgotten to deactivate the "tag."

Mr. Sam and I had a conversation in the hallway where I explained to him the merits of the technology. I explained that the system had performed very well for other retailers, in some cases reducing their shoplifting by half. For Walmart, that represented millions of dollars. He said "keep trying" and gave me no indication that he was interested or would pursue this opportunity.

Mr. Sam's legacy consists of many things, and one aspect of that legacy was that his mind was razor-sharp, and he was extremely good with detail. He knew full well at the time of our conversation that any solution that could reduce his "shrinkage" by half would save Walmart tens of millions of dollars.

A very close friend of mine at Walmart, who was responsible for Walmart's loss prevention department, attended a meeting shortly after my hallway conversation with Mr. Sam. In the meeting, Walmart executive leadership discussed the merits of the new technology along with the dozens of other topics that the executive leadership team discussed daily, and no one was in favor of pursuing the solution. They assumed the efforts needed to deter shoplifters might upset good paying customers.

In the world of Walmart, the customer was priority #1. Mr. Sam's quotes are prominent throughout the Walmart home office in Bentonville, Arkansas, as well as in every store in the world (10,000+ at last count, and at 485 billion dollars, they are the largest company in the world).

One brief but powerful quote reads: "The Customer, The Associate, The Shareholder, in that order!" Mr. Sam stood in the back of that board room, which was called the Quail Room. A bronze of Mr. Sam's most beloved bird dog, Ol' Roy, the face of one of the best-selling dog food brands in the world, sat atop a driftwood table centerpiece with several bronze quail perched on the wood. (The quail were likely birds shot by Mr. Sam himself on his ranch in Falfurrias, Texas.)

Mr. Sam, eating a tuna fish sandwich wrapped in wax paper, said to the executive committee, "How will you know if you don't try?" With that one question, Mr. Sam and Walmart changed the fortunes of not only a single company but an entire industry—by trying something new that they were unsure of and uncomfortable with. The decision wound up being a very wise decision for Walmart. The technology did, in fact, help them reduce their inventory shrinkage, the technology did, in fact, deter would-be shoplifters, and it did not offend their good paying customers.

Because the decision to embrace change was successful, I'm sure other decisions were made along the same lines with other technologies and or solutions. The technology that they tried was started in a couple of stores, as Walmart will often do with new changes. Today, it has become over a billion-dollar relationship between Walmart and the technology provider. Walmart has grown to over $485 billion dollars in sales worldwide, and the technology provider as well as countless ancillary solution providers were afforded the opportunity to grow right along with Walmart. Because Mr. Sam, the visionary leader not afraid of change, tried something new and different, because he challenged his executive leadership team to "try" because the technology performed as advertised, the decision to embrace change worked on that day!

The secondary theme to this story of Mr. Sam embracing and encouraging change is the importance of taking risks. Embracing change should not be confused with blind faith, or simple gambling. Mr. Sam and his leadership team left very little to chance; they demanded visibility to "how" we would deploy the technology and "what" might be the expected reaction from their customers and associates. We built contingency plans for the multitude of outcomes for the numerous folks who would come into contact with this technology. We performed a POC (Proof of Concept) for which we gathered reams of data. Then we tweaked the processes and various elements of the POC based on data gathered and pivoted into a pilot deployment. From the pilot deployment, we gathered more data. We analyzed the data and improved upon our pilot deployments to begin a full roll-out across the enterprise.

As leaders, we should not fear change. We can't afford to take unnecessary chances without thinking through the potential outcomes. We must be diligent soldiers of detail. We must control what we can control and when implementing change, make sure that the change you embrace is the change you have crafted, as much as market forces allow.

Do not fear change!

CHAPTER 9

Reality of Personal Change versus the Perception of Change

by Joe DeSensi

Part 1: Change-in-Perception Lag Time

In quantum physics, light has a dual nature. It is a photon in a single moment of time, but it is also the wave of the path it has taken, which defines the light's color and other qualities.

In my graduate classes on leadership, I have been talking a lot about reality versus perceived reality. In day-to-day life, we assume most people experience the world with the same convictions and interpretations as ourselves. Of course, just by looking (for instance) at all of the news organizations that exist, we see that people can have radically different interpretations of the same event. Despite our usual assumption, we can soundly say that we don't all experience the world in exactly the same way.

With the understanding that things are perceived differently, we should look at how we believe we are being perceived. We build up a track record—if you will, a trend analysis over time—in other people's heads that is slow to move towards the good but, unfortunately, can turn quickly towards the bad. In our own minds, we have moments in time that truly change us: an amazing book that we read, listening to a speaker or a TED talk that make some things clearer, time working with a coach or mentor, or even just the trials of a rough year or project.

If we think about the example of light—reality as we experience it, and the things that change us, occur rather quickly as moments in time. We are perceived as changing not after the changes, but only after we show, through our consistent actions, that we have changed. For example: if a doctor gives us bad news about our cholesterol or our body fat, it is not directly after the resolution to improve our health that our bodies gets better, but after we've actually worked out for a few months, dropped some weight, and cleaned up our eating habits that our bodies begin to show the benefits.

Similarly, if we have had trouble communicating and we go to a coach, counselor, or class, it is not the certificate from the course that will change people's perceptions of us. It is us putting the learning into practice over time and slowly reworking the perception of who we are to the people with whom we interact. A change in reality can happen quickly; a change in perceived reality, as by coworkers or teammates, can take quite a bit of time depending on how long the old perceived reality has stood.

When coming back from a meeting facilitation class and finding that people don't immediately jump into the new ways that you would like, it should not be a surprise (even if it's frustrating). Your team members are basing their behaviors on everything they have known to date, and it could take a while before they start to perceive the "New You" that truly wants their input, as opposed to the "Old You" that did not want to hear any dissent or different ideas.

Understanding the difference—between (A) the moment in time that changes you and (B) the perceptions of those around you based on your track record— is important so that you do not give up on a new idea or way of handling yourself just because it doesn't produce immediate results. You didn't start here either; you got here. So give others a bit of a chance to catch up with the New You.

Part 2: Projecting Success for Self and Others

Henry Ford once said, "Whether you think you can or you think you can't, you're right." There is real wisdom in this notion of belief manifesting itself in reality (self-fulfilling prophecies, the Pygmalion effect, the placebo effect, etc.). So many people have low opinions of their abilities; this plays out when applying for jobs and also when it comes time for a promotion or higher position. How you feel about yourself projects through your posture, your word choice, your tone, and so on. If you don't believe in you, why should someone else? You know you better than anyone else. As the authority on yourself, you give indications of how you should be perceived. If you question your convictions or second-guess yourself, then it follows suit that others should as well. If you sound confident and are clear in message and direction, then others will perceive that you know what you are doing.

Perception of reality is an important concept for communicating confidence and competency on an empathetic level. Notice: if you have a lot of confidence in yourself but appear unsure when you communicate, people will perceive you as unsure. Yet even if you're not completely certain of what you're saying or doing, but present yourself as assured and confident, people will perceive you as such. In other words, "fake it 'til you make it" is not only a good way to help yourself believe in your real abilities, but it instills more confidence in those following you or leading you.

In coaching sessions, I hear very capable people present a version of themselves far less than what my observations and performance data supports. After a short discussion, they realize that their current view of self is extreme. Here are some tips towards a better self-image which will, in turn, create a better public image:

Make a list of things at which you excel and be confident in using it. We keep our shortcomings close at hand. It is not as natural to take a personal inventory of strengths. So do that. List the things that you do well or come naturally to you. Go ahead and list the things upon which you need to improve, but go the next step and create a plan for improvement. A deficit with a plan and solution does not weigh as heavily on our self-perception as a deficit by itself.

Base new opportunities on your potential rather than your past. People are quick to tell you about self-doubts or past failures. If that is not you anymore, it isn't relevant. The past is only useful for lessons that we can learn, from both success and failure. You usually learn more from failures than from success-es—and if you don't learn from failure, we have bigger problems to fix than self-confidence.

Find a cheerleader. All of us have a friend or coworker that sees the best ver-sion of who we think we are. Don't abuse it, but when you're having a crisis of confidence, or if you need a boost before an interview or presentation, go get a fix. That's what friends are for.

Conclusion

Part 1 of this chapter examines the gap between the changes we see in ourselves and the changes we want others to see. One thing we didn't discuss is that sometimes others perceive changes in us (either good or bad) when we perceive ourselves as having stayed the same. In Part 2, projecting the desired image can expedite both believing in the internal change and having others believe it. The key to understanding both of these ideas is understanding that change is slow. It is perceived at different rates and in different ways, and unless one is intentional about changing and communicating that change to others, per-ceived change is slower or, in some cases, goes unnoticed.

As a final idea: think of yourself as a brand. First, think about who you want to be. What is it that you want to define you? Next, how are you going to com-municate that to others? (How will you believe it yourself?) Everything about you, from your resting facial expressions to how you speak to how you define your future comes from envisioning your future self, becoming that self, and then making sure that others see the new and improved you.

CHAPTER 10

Do What Your Career Can Stand

by Tom Roach

John Wayne as Hondo said, "A man ought to do what he thinks is right." What does that mean in a professional context? We will explore three basic assumptions concerning doing what you think is right: (1) knowing what is right, (2) having an accurate viewpoint, and (3) taking action. In the last section, we will examine six elements to consider when you assess a work environment.

First, "to do what you think is right" assumes you know the difference between right and wrong. Your understanding of right and wrong likely began as a child when you first understood the word *no*. From there, it probably grew into a system of ethics based on formal and informal training. These may have included family, school, and a faith-based institution. For me, Dad was a school teacher, and the family all went to church together. There was a near-seamless transition between these segments. Ideals presented in formal settings were reinforced with colloquialisms from various family members:

- "Treat people like you want to be treated."
- "Don't do anything during the day that will keep you up at night."
- "Nothing good happens away from home after midnight."
- "Your actions reflect on the family."
- "Do what's right especially when no one is looking; it will be easier when they are."

- "Tell the truth; it's easier to remember."
- "Roll with pigs and you will smell just like them."

We work under the assumption that as a professional, you have a basic set of values suitable for a work environment.

Thomas Jefferson, author of the Declaration of Independence and the Statute of Virginia for Religious Freedom, third President of the United States, and founder of the University of Virginia, was a major proponent of learning. He understood that public education was essential to establishing a baseline of acceptable behaviors.

> *"The objects of... primary education [which] determine its character and limits [are]: To give to every citizen the information he needs for the transaction of his own business; to enable him to calculate for himself, and to express and preserve his ideas, his contracts and accounts in writing; to improve, by reading, his morals and faculties; to understand his duties to his neighbors and country, and to discharge with competence the functions confided to him by either; to know his rights; to exercise with order and justice those he retains, to choose with discretion the fiduciary of those he delegates; and to notice their conduct with diligence, with candor and judgment; and in general, to observe with intelligence and faithfulness all the social relations under which he shall be placed."*
> —*Report for University of Virginia (1818)*

From President Jefferson's statement, we see the basic premise of formal education is to make us better citizens, better neighbors, and better stewards. Schools accomplish this mandate with the introduction of conduct standards in a social setting, namely the classroom; introduction to letters, words, and numbers and basic logic through mathematical equations; then, finally, tests of knowledge that typically focus on the student's ability to recall information. Elementary schools have more structure and are more prescriptive; as students progress, they receive more autonomy in high school and have an increasingly difficult curriculum. The increasing difficulty includes a greater volume of information, more critical thinking, and more complex logic. For students that continue their education in a collegiate setting, they experience a self-guided educational program, with the expectation that they have a firm grasp of the basic information and can make more complex logical connections. Universities have a near-autonomous construct with basic standards and then the professor's guidelines for the class environment. For the student, the question changes from "what must I do?" to "what can I do?"

Second, to "do the right thing" assumes your view of right and wrong is in fact accurate, that it is correct in detail or fact, and that it is exact. The definition of "accuracy" may vary between cultures, industries, or organizations. Tipping is considered rude in Japan; showing the bottom of your feet to someone from the Middle East is an insult; people from rural areas of the United States have larger personal space expectations than those from urban areas. It's important to have an "accurate" understanding of how right and wrong has its own rules in different contexts. Every organization has a culture and accepted behaviors or beliefs that, whether formal or informal, set expectations. This culture and expectations can be expressed in ways ranging from the spoken word for a small group to reams of written procedures, policies, and manuals in large bureaucracies such as the Army.

Lastly, and most importantly, to "do the right thing" assumes you are willing to act on your convictions, or your fixed and firmly-held beliefs. You may find yourself in a position where your personal values conflict with the organization's or your direct supervisor's. Acting on your convictions may be extraordinarily challenging as you balance the need to pay your bills and take care of your family while not selling your soul or sacrificing your family on the career altar. Your convictions may require you to "take the hard right over the easy left" when you come to that critical crossroad. Avoiding a battle by forsaking your convictions will not likely yield you peace; you will simply move the pain from some external manifestation to an internal turmoil. Unfortunately, we're all not independently wealthy, so working is a requirement. While the questions below are not an all-inclusive list, they provide some general guidelines to consider before you accept a position.

Assessing the Work Environment

Know yourself. Beyond your height, weight, food preferences, the clothes you wear, and how you like your coffee, what do you know about yourself? What is your color, number, or letter set? Are you a morning person or do you peak in the afternoon? Are you most productive working by yourself or as part of a small team? Do you need general guidance or very specific instructions? What is your tolerance for risk? What is your conflict resolution style? Do you need quiet or music at a low drone in the background?

Values. Understand, to the fullest extent possible, the formal and informal values of the organization and your boss. Values are generally accepted as the operating philosophy that guides internal and external relationships. Corporate, or core, values must be more than a list of individual values, but should build upon them. The formal values will probably be obvious, published in writing, maybe even posted on the wall or the website. They may make a snappy acronym; they may be trite. Are the formal values just as obvious in action? That is, are they walking the talk or just talking the talk?

In a manufacturing environment, are they shipping sub-quality goods just to meet the production numbers, or are they only shipping quality product? What if the value conflict is not with corporate or the team, but rather with the specific leader for whom you would work? Is there someone on the team that has said, "When you hear the boss say this, they really mean that"? If so, you may have identified a difference between the formal and informal values of the corporation, or at least differences in values among the management team.

Interaction. Talk to those with whom you would work and, if possible, observe the work environment. How does the workforce interact with one another? How do they communicate verbally, in writing, in email, in meetings, outside meetings, and through their body language? The focus here is not the bureaucratic requirements, necessarily, but the personal interactions. Do you get the sense people like their jobs and the people with whom they work? Does their body language reveal tension between co-workers or disdain for boss, management, or the company? Ideally, the team will be courteous, professional, and friendly. They may eat together at lunch, share some of their outside interests in conversation, or even spend some time together after work hours.

Leaders. Identifying the formal leaders should be fairly easy; identifying the informal leaders may not. In general, informal leaders are perceived by those within the organization as having reputation or experience that makes their voice worth hearing.

Remember the basketball movie *Hoosiers*? When the Hickory townspeople are ready to fire Coach Norman Dale, Jimmy Chitwood, the best basketball player in town, asks to speak to the assembled crowd. His statement is a profound as it is brief: he will continue to play basketball, but only if Norman Dale remains coach. Having already voted to fire him, a new vote is cast with near-unanimous consent for Coach Dale to continue.

Although not every informal leader will have as dramatic an effect as Jimmy, they will all likely have the same ability to sway the group's opinion or even the formal leader's decision. Here are some questions to help identify them:

- Who talks the least but says the most?
- Who is considered the subject matter expert?
- If you had to ask professional advice of only one person here, who would it be and why?

- Who has the boss' ear and why?
- Does the boss single out any one person for input, especially outside a group setting?

The Boss. What can you observe about the boss' leadership? Does he or she tell you (1) what he or she wants accomplished, (2) what he or she wants you to do, or (3) how he or she wants you to do it? Notice there is a distinct difference in each of these approaches, and the approach he or she chooses identifies the amount of flexibility the boss gives the employees to accomplish tasks.

Does (s)he explain the plan so you see the larger picture and how your part plays into it? Does (s)he ask for input about what to do or how to do it?

How does the boss communicate and how can you expect to communicate with him or her? Tact matters. Depending on how long you've known the boss and the strength of the professional relationship, you may be more direct; however, you should not be curt. When in doubt about what the boss wants, ask questions. Make sure you have a very clear understanding of the situation and his/her guidance. Is the boss receptive to such questions? If not, do you get the impression the boss is thinking, "If I have to tell you how to do your job…" or "I don't care how you do it, it's yours to screw up"?

Success. How do people gauge success? Are there set metrics concerning productivity? Are expectations clearly communicated, or does the boss provide some vague guidance about when the project might be due? Are the expectations communicated in writing to include the expected duration of projects? Is there are a weekly meeting and does it have a regular cadence of accountability? Is the appraisal system formal? Are performance reviews annual, semi-annual, or quarterly? Are bonuses tied to performance or does everyone get the same bonus?

Turnover. What is the turnover rate, both voluntary and involuntary, especially among your likely peer group? What's the average length of service among your peer group? People join a company for the pay and benefits, but stay because of relationships; generally speaking, the immediate supervisor has the greatest impact, positive or negative, on employee voluntary turnover. (Involuntary turnover is more an indication of how well the company operates, how well it forecasted changes in product demand, and how well it managed staffing level changes.)

Turnover has a cost associated with it that varies based on positional skill requirements. Thirty to forty percent turnover in unskilled hourly positions may be acceptable; twenty percent in skilled positions may not. Costs may include training requirements, lower productivity, severance pay, advertising for replacements, or work hours related to interviewing candidates. High turnover rates may not be a cause for alarm but should cause you to ask some probing questions before accepting a position.

Work is like any other relationship; it takes effort and effective communication on both sides. Knowing yourself and knowing your work environment are critical to your long-term success. However, if the relationship gets out of balance, you may have to make a change. If the imbalance is due to a moral dilemma in which you find yourself, don't sacrifice your integrity for your company or your boss. You have to live with yourself regardless of where you work. It will take a toll on you and your family—so, as best you can, have a plan financially, personally and professionally, that gives you flexibility. If necessary, be willing to walk away on your own terms.

SECTION III

Coaching and Organizational Development

When we lead, we hope to set a good example for others and exemplify some of the attributes that we would like to see in our followers. Coaching and organizational development are a little bit different, as they aim to develop better leaders and better followers. This section of the book addresses trends and techniques in coaching and Human Resources for developing talent inside of an organization.

Whitney and Hope take a data-driven approach to developing a coaching culture in an organization in **"Creating an Evidence-Based Coaching Culture."**

Joe offers the first of two chapters on communication and empathy, **"A Lesson in Winning: How Are They Keeping Score?"** which explores how empathy and others' metrics of success are important to crafting a message.

Jeff Nally looks at leadership as coaching, and explains why to ask the right questions rather than dispense advice, in **"Great Leaders Have All the Right ~~Answers~~ Questions."**

Alonzo explores the "Can," the "Will," and the "Fit" of hiring the best employee for a position in **"Three Questions to Help You Hire the Best-Fit Employee."** (Adapted from his book *Hiring Made Easy as PIE*.)

Joe's second piece on communication and empathy, **"Empathy and Ends-Based Communication: You Haven't Said It If They Haven't Heard It!"** changes how we define effective communication—by focusing on what is *understood* rather than what is said.

CHAPTER 11

Creating an Evidence-Based Coaching Culture

by Hope Zoeller and Whitney Martin

Coaching means different things to different people and can vary in its effectiveness depending on how it is carried out. How can you be intentional in creating a coaching culture to ensure a maximum level of success? How can you incorporate objective data into the coaching process to increase impact?

The benefits of developing a coaching culture are vast. According to a survey conducted by the Institute of Leadership and Management, 95% of respondents had coaching experiences that directly benefitted the organization, and 96% experienced benefits to the individual. A wide range of improvements included communication and interpersonal skills, leadership and management, conflict resolution, personal confidence, attitudes and motivation, management performance, and preparation for a new role or promotion.

So, how do you create this type of high-performance coaching culture in your organization?

1. **Define "coaching."** Coaching isn't telling people what to do differently. Unfortunately, many organizations still perceive coaching as a corrective tool for poor performance. However, good coaching is about achieving a high-performance culture, not managing a low-performance one. Coaching is a cooperative, interactive process of managers and employees working together on improved performance and leadership development. In a

coaching culture, there is regular feedback and communication to coach the employee to sustain, improve, or correct behaviors and skills. To sustain this culture, managers need to be committed to taking a coaching role with employees. As an organization, you need to explicitly define this with your managers and then train them on how to effectively perform this role.

2. **Develop a shared vision for the coaching culture.** Once a coaching culture is in place, senior leaders need to define what results the organization can achieve, what people will feel as a result, and ultimately how coaching will influence positive behavior changes—with an observable and measurable impact—on the business. One example of a coaching culture vision is: "To create an environment that elevates performance by integrating coaching techniques and principles into the organization and by aligning coaching with the business strategy by educating and engaging leaders in the coaching process."

3. **Get senior leader buy-in and participation.** Without support from the top, a coaching culture is doomed to fail before it begins. Once you identify an executive level sponsor(s), you need to create measurements for change. Once on board, senior leaders need to receive coaching to truly understand the power of coaching and to fully support it. However, it should not be limited to senior executives; while the focus of coaching may vary, all levels of employees—definitely all managers and leaders—in an organization can benefit from coaching.

4. **Integrate measurement tools.** Various measurement and assessment tools can play an invaluable role in several parts of the coaching process. Self-report assessments of personality, mental ability, passions and strengths, leadership style, or numerous other constructs can provide insight into how well the leader is "matched" to their current job. Do they get to fully utilize their strengths and passions? Or, on the other

hand, are they frequently required to behave in ways that are significantly different from how they are "hard-wired"?

For example, consider a manager who is typically unassertive and conflict-avoidant. Perhaps they demonstrate a "servant leadership" approach, which can be highly effective. However, it is likely also difficult for this leader to be firm or confrontational, which are necessary behaviors from time to time. Coaching can help this leader develop adaptive behaviors to help him or her be more effective when the situation mandates more assertiveness, even if that is not this leader's natural tendency.

Such tools may also reveal, if a leader is required to "be someone they are not" for such a large portion of each day, that perhaps the job is not a good fit. In this case, assessments may help identify a role (inside or outside of the organization) where the leader will be better positioned for success.

Another tool that can provide essential data in the coaching process is 360-degree feedback. 360-degree feedback tools are designed to solicit feedback from critical "stakeholders" on the leader's success, including their boss, peers, direct reports, customers, board members, and so on. 360 data can provide essential information at both the "micro" and "macro" level. At the "micro" or individual level, the information gleaned from a 360 can form the basis of a coaching strategy and individual development plan. It can answer questions like:

- **Is this leader's self-perception in line with the experience of those he or she works with?** If the leader's self-perception is significantly higher or lower than those they work with, coaching efforts may not be well-received until the leader learns to accept "reality."
- **Are this leader and their boss in alignment on the focus and priorities of this person's job?** For example: if the leader thinks he or she should be focused on delivering results and demonstrating technical expertise,

but their boss thinks they need to be delegating and building the capabilities of their team, performance expectations will never be met due to a disagreement about focus and strategy. This information can become the basis for highly productive conversations about expectations.

- **What specific behaviors are contributing to the perception that a particular competency is an area for development?** If a 360 reveals that a leader is perceived as a poor listener, for example, what should the development plan be? There are innumerable options for developing listening skills. However, a good 360 tool will provide more granular, more actionable feedback—perhaps revealing that the leader often interrupts, or doesn't solicit ideas and opinions from all members of the group equally. With that level of specificity, creating an efficient development plan for behavioral change is much easier.

- **After coaching has occurred, is progress being made?** 360s can serve as a "pre-post" measure to determine both strengths and weaknesses before the coaching, and then determine if the leader was able to "move the needle" sufficiently in mission-critical areas.

If 360-degree feedback is gathered on multiple leaders in the organization, the data can be examined in aggregate to answer important "macro" level questions as well. For example, are there certain developmental needs that appear to be systemic in the organization? If so, group training may be an effective development strategy.

Macro-level 360 data can also reveal whether leaders' strengths align with the organization's culture, priorities, and unique selling proposition. For instance, if the organization is a high-growth, high-tech company that thrives on innovation, but many of the leaders struggle with "thinking creatively" (as revealed by 360 data), this could be a crippling deficit.

Coaching should not happen in isolation. The greatest impact can be achieved when organizations connect coaching to the strategic plan. This requires a commitment to the initiative for a minimum of two to three years. Senior leadership also needs to agree upon return on investment measures; these measures must be relevant to the organization, connected to business strategy, and able to be tracked effectively.

For those organizations willing to embark on the journey, the impact on business can be tremendous, dramatically impacting your culture and your people for the better. It's amazing what individuals can achieve with the right level of support and development. When coaching is successfully integrated into the culture of an organization, it creates a competitive advantage and unlocks untapped talent and potential.

CHAPTER 12

A Lesson in Winning:
How Are They Keeping Score?

by Joe DeSensi

People often tell me stories about having arguments with their bosses. The person thinks he or she has a good idea or is alerting the manager to an important issue, and whatever it is the manager just doesn't see it. Then, the person says to me that this sort of thing happens all the time. The first piece of advice I usually give is that, if this happens all the time, you are allowed to be frustrated by it, but you are not allowed to be surprised by it. Similar inputs should have similar outputs. Next, I tell them to try to think of different ways to frame the inputs, since we know the current approach is not working. The first step in this process is figuring out how the person is keeping score. Put another way: what is that person's grading rubric?

Knowing the Rubric

Take, for example, Olympic gymnastics. There are many, many ways the athletes are judged, such as time limit, staying within boundaries, scoring opportunities, restrictions, basic competencies, and so on. The judges, the coaches, the athletes, and many of the spectators know the ins and outs of each tenth of a point given or taken; when there are rule changes, it ripples through the community very quickly.

On the other hand, there is cricket. As an American sportsman, I am fairly certain that cricket is a game invented to make American sports enthusiasts confused and upset. Really, I say that because *I* could never be a decent cricket player without far more understanding of the game, its scoring, and its rules (if, indeed, the game isn't a hoax perpetrated on North America). I might swing hard, run hard, and throw hard, as I learned to in other games, but I don't know how to score properly in cricket, much less how to win.

Here's another example from academia. In the graduate school class I teach on Strategic Planning, I give students the rubric for the final presentation. Students have ten minutes (plus or minus two) to sell me on the issues from their strategic analyses, which were their class projects. There are specific grading points for the opening, the conclusion, the materials, making the case for their issues, and some general presentation best practices. Sometimes, I have students who are unhappy about how they scored, and sometimes they'll then make a comparison to someone who, in their opinion, gave a lesser presentation. In those cases, I ask what made it lesser; they might note fewer slides, or more reading from index cards by the presenter. I say, "OK, so that's how you would keep score. But let's look at the rubric I gave you and see how I was keeping score."

In the classic comedy *Caddyshack*, a fellow golfer is trying to get Chevy Chase to divulge how well he normally plays. Chevy says that he doesn't keep score. The other golfer asks him how he measures himself against other golfers. The 6'4" Chase responds, "By height." The metrics of success by which people are judged in a given place don't necessarily have to be fair, don't have to be well-communicated, and don't even have to be the most important metrics by which something should be judged. If you have no control over the scoring rubric, you must play your best hand with the rules that are set for you. Just remember that, if you are playing poker and are dealt a hand great for rummy, it is unlikely that the rest of the table will allow you to claim victory by rummy rules.

This is true in business as well. Some people only play the game of business and measure success in it the way they wish score were kept. So they say: if I have the right answer, why does it matter if I say it in a gruff tone? If I hit my dates, why should I care if the 360 shows my relationship with my team is strained? If no one is quitting or protesting, so what if I'm a little over budget? Why are these things important, they ask? Because the judge that will score their rubrics—and determine the winners—says it is. Why are my relationships with team members important if the customer is happy with me? Because the person that fills out my performance review says it is—period.

Sometimes, it can take experience and trial-and-error to figure out what some of the "secret" grading line items are. For these, it might take some time before you earn full points in every category. Other times, the rules are explicit: you need to hit your dates without any more delays. You need to stay within budget even if quality suffers. You need to improve your relationship with your employees if you want to be considered for a promotion. When you are told point-blank what the line items on a rubric are, disregarding them is your choice alone.

It might not be fair. In fact, if someone tells you to do something unethical, you might deliberately choose to forego those points because of how you choose to play the game. You can feel good about the choices that you make, but you can't be surprised if you lose those points.

This does not mean you should do everything you are told to do regardless of strategic impact or ethics. It means this: know how the score will be kept, then make conscious decisions about the points for which you choose to play and the points you decide to forego.

This also builds a sense of empathy with one of the key people to reviewing your performance, your short-term raises, and possibly your short-term promotions. Just trying to do good work without thinking of how work will be evaluated might lead to some unintentional successes, but strategic successes go into a project, a job, or a quarter knowing in advance what winning looks like. How are they keeping score?

Here are some more examples of "scoring principles" that might be counter-intuitive on the surface:

- Being wrong in the correct way is sometimes better than being right. Results are rarely the only success criterion. Sometimes the right process can be more important in the long run than "doing whatever it takes" for a short-term win.
- Being the best at what you do might not put you first in line for a promotion. Promotions and management can be more about enabling others, developing personal relationships, supporting the goals of superiors, and playing well with coworkers. We don't do our jobs in a vacuum. We work within a context where output is only one metric. Synergy, morale, employee retention, and other group dynamics can be as important as individual output.
- Helping areas or individuals that are struggling isn't always best. We don't want to leave our teammates hanging, but regularly taking up slack and masking team or individual deficiencies means that future planning might be inaccurate and at risk. Masking areas of weakness might seem like service to your team, but it can mask real competency and capacity issues. It is OK to help others, but only if it is broadcasted so that management can plan better going forward.
- "I was told what is important, so I am on solid footing for the life of a project." Unfortunately, things change. It is good to regularly check in, both to provide status updates and to recalibrate your metrics of success. Sometimes we assume that information critical to our departments or projects will be offered to us, unsolicited—but I personally have had information communicated to me as an aside, almost on accident, that would have meant failure for the project if I hadn't heard it.

Remember that managers are people too. Liking them and being liked by them makes their days go more smoothly. This does not mean a nice person that regularly missed dates is "just fine" and needs no coaching or performance enhancements—but this also does not mean that a gruff, hard-to-talk-to employee that meets his or her dates is acceptable, either.

Sometimes budget is fixed. Sometimes, the timeline is most important even if additional, unbudgeted resources are required to hit milestones. It always depends.

Here is the key that will open the treasures of Arabia: **ask.** Probe to see what is really important. Don't assume you will be told what is most important. Force-rank the priorities and ask those keeping score if you have your metrics in order. Many of us assume the standards of success, and only sometimes experience or luck will get us through perfectly. In new circumstances, or with new management or teammates, it's better to be explicit than to ever be in doubt.

Last little tidbit: As part of the chartering process of a department or a project, I always have people create an Assumptions Subsidiary Management report (a way to formally document the "why" behind "what" is decided). I think something less formal should be done as you calibrate and track the less official rubrics of success.

Remember that being right is not enough—you have to be perceived as right. Feeling like you won may not mean that everyone else perceives a victory for you. Try to delay playing as long as possible until you get the scoring rubric!

CHAPTER 13

Great Leaders Have All the Right ~~Answers~~ Questions

by Jeff Nally

> *"Questions wake people up. They prompt new ideas.*
> *They show people new places, new ways of doing things."*
> — *Michael Marquardt*

Tom is the customer service manager of a new mail-order pharmacy company, and he has a big problem.

He leads a team of customer service supervisors at the call center where customers submit prescriptions, request refills, and ask questions about their medicines. The calls are backing up, phones aren't getting answered promptly, customer service representatives are taking too long to answer questions on the phone, and complaints are starting to pile up.

He looks at the quality and efficiency report for the first week of operations, and it looks like someone spilled red paint all over the report. Almost every bar in the graph is red—an indicator that quality standards are not being met and inefficiencies are everywhere.

Tom created all the customer service processes, scripts, and training for the representatives. He and his supervisors hired experienced customer service representatives who know how to handle tough customers. He can't figure out why his methods aren't working. The customer service supervisors don't know what to do. They walk into Tom's office and say, "Tell us how to fix this mess!" Tom has always been "the manager with all the answers." He feels compelled to fix everything on his own, especially when his team asks him to solve complex problems. This time, however, he's not sure about the right answer. He's not sure there is just one answer to solve all the problems that are occurring in the call center. He has a few guesses, but he's not certain they will lead to the right solutions.

Tom thinks about blurting out a laundry list of improbable solutions, and then he stops himself. He remembers what he learned from his executive coach: "Leaders don't always lead at their best with answers. Great leaders have all the right questions."

Tom decides this is the time to ask all the right questions.

Leaders Have All The Answers ... Right?

Leaders are expected to have answers: all the answers, all the time. All too often, organizations rely on leaders to provide solutions, which can be an overwhelming role for leaders to play. Teams and organizations rely on the leader's expertise and know-how to solve problems. That's what we want leaders to do, right? Yes—if there's low risk in having only the leader's point of view and solution. Yes—when the team needs to learn from the leader's expertise. Yes—when there's one, clear solution to a simple problem.

However, there are situations when there simply isn't a clear answer or simple decision that will solve a problem. There may be several possible solutions or no viable solution at all. The risk of implementing an ineffective solution is high, and a negative impact on employees, customers, and the organization would be likely.

A leader's greater contribution, however, is not always being the go-to person for a solution. The greater contribution is asking the right questions to help individuals and teams think more clearly on their own. It's a prime opportunity to teach teams to create solutions and build their capability to lead through tough situations.

What Are the Right Questions?

Tom and the supervisors could have told the customer service representatives to talk faster so they could take more calls. They could have retrained representatives on the call procedures and reinforced the service standards. There's no guarantee, however, that these solutions would solve the problems on that bloodied report.

The next time you're in a situation like Tom's, ask the right questions. Ask great coaching questions.

Coaching questions are designed to prompt new thinking, insights, and ideas. They quiet down the voice of experience in the leader's head that assumes the action he took in the past will be the same solution to fix the current problem. Coaching questions give leaders a few moments to get clear in their thinking before they charge ahead with acts that may not solve the problem.

Tom takes a deep breath and tells his supervisors, "This situation is too complex for me to assume I have the right answer, or that what we tried in the past will be the right solution. Let's answer some questions that will generate better solutions and next steps." The managers agree, and Tom begins to ask some coaching questions:

What do we really, really want? Ask this gut-check question to find out if the team is focused on useful, meaningful outcomes. Perhaps they are focused on the wrong goal or outcome. Help teams refocus on what they really, really want, and they can agree on the goal before going further.

When Tom asks the supervisors, "What do we really, really want?" they explain that they want customers to get the right prescription, at the right time, with the right guidance, to improve their health. They agree this is the goal and outcome that is important to customers and to their pharmacy company.

What is working correctly? This coaching question helps leaders get clear on what's working as expected. When problems arise, the emotional center of the brain goes on the defensive and stress levels increase. These emotions shut down the parts of the brain that generate new insights and ideas. Calm the emotional center of the brain by paying attention to what is working. Build confidence in the team by letting them identify what is operating as expected. This also tells leaders what they do not have to pay attention to for now.

Tom's supervisors tell him that the phone systems are working as expected, calls are coming in, and calls are routed to customer service representative as soon as they are available for the next call. Computer systems are working. Employees arrive to work on time, and there's no excessive absenteeism. The reporting systems are working, and we know exactly where our quality and efficiency problems are.

What are we noticing when we look beyond the red flags? Leaders get focused on exception reports, red flags, and alarms that go off when processes and systems fail. If leaders keep paying attention to the alarms, they are less likely to notice signals other than the red flags and less likely to learn while fixing problems. Turn off the alarms, set aside the exception report, and discover what leaders see, hear, know, experience, and learn.

Tom's supervisors set down the report covered in red bar graphs and they started talking about what they experienced in the call center that week. One supervisor noted that Kathy was talking with a customer who had seven different prescriptions, and it took a long time to tell the customer about the potential side effects of each drug. Another supervisor noticed in the customer demographics report that 60% of the customers calling in the previous week were over 65 years old—a lot of seniors with multiple prescriptions. Another supervisor pointed out that the call center had the heaviest call volume between 10 AM and 4 PM; there were fewer calls on hold or unanswered before 10 AM and after 4 PM.

What are five directions that can move us closer to potential solutions? Identify five directions to consider before jumping into action (I'll explain why five in a moment). Leaders are likely to observe one or two data points and start taking actions that may not solve the problem. Generate options and potential directions before deciding which directions to explore.

It's like checking the GPS before taking a long road trip. There may be several options to get you to your destination, and you want to consider each one before just jumping in the car and heading down the road. The GPS may indicate a route that maximizes highways and interstates to save time; there may be a scenic route that takes you through several national parks; there may also be a route that avoids construction and closed roads. If you don't assess what route works best for your needs, you won't have the best road trip you can. So identify and examine several directions before deciding to take action!

Why five directions? Why not consider just two or three? I prescribe five because asking leaders to generate five directions requires them to think more deeply. The first two or three ideas may be "low-hanging fruit," easy for their minds to grab. Asking leaders to generate five ideas requires them to think beyond the immediate possibilities.

Tom's supervisors start offering directions to explore. One supervisor says, "We could check this week's call reports to see when people in different age groups are calling most frequently. If seniors are calling between 10:00 AM and 4:00 PM, when are other age groups likely to call? How might that inform a solution?"

Another supervisor suggests: "We can determine which customer service representatives are completing calls within our target service time of four minutes and ask them how they achieve that target. There may be a solution we can apply to all customer service representatives." Another supervisor then added the suggestion that they check the different length of time of calls for customers with one prescription, between two and five prescriptions, and those with over six prescriptions, since the number of prescriptions a customer has could be key to their solution.

Another supervisor says, "Let's look at the years of experience for each customer service representative to see if those with more experience conclude calls more quickly than those with less experience."

Another supervisor says, "Let's listen to some of the recorded of calls that lasted longer than four minutes. We might learn something that helps us shorten the call time."

See how they're starting to generate useful ideas?

What have we not thought about that could move us closer to potential solutions? There's power in asking leaders what they have *not* thought about, considered, or included in the conversation. This question moves attention away from the immediate, current thinking. Asking the 'not' question triggers the brain to think about gaps or missing pieces to the puzzle.

Tom asks the question, and one supervisor says, "We haven't thought about ways the call system technology can help us solve the problem." The other supervisors agree that checking the technology capabilities would be a useful consideration.

Tom thinks all of these ideas are worth an hour or two of exploration. He asks the supervisors to explore these directions and return with observations in two hours.

What needs to exist so we can take action? This coaching question helps leaders determine resources necessary to take action. It helps expand their thinking to consider:

- Who can help?
- What needs to be accomplished?
- When does it need to occur?
- How much time will be required?
- Where will this take place?
- What resources will we need?

The supervisors then return with their observations, and they propose some actions to solve their problem.

They find that customers over sixty-five years old have an average of seven prescriptions. Seniors know their prescriptions very well, but they ask lots of questions about side effects and the interactions between the drugs. They want the customer service representative to confirm what the prescription label says. They call during the day when they are not busy doing other things with family or friends. These calls average eight minutes, twice the length of time that set for efficiency standards per call.

The supervisors proposed the following solution: "Let's put 60 percent of our representatives on calls for customers over age 65 between 10:00 AM and 4:00 PM, and change the efficiency standard to an average of eight minutes per call.

We will direct all other calls to the remaining representatives, and determine if those calls can be resolved within the four minute efficiency standard."

Tom asks them: "What needs to exist so we can take action on your recommendation?" The team identifies all the people and resources they will need to get going. They head for the door when Tom calls them back and says he has one more question:

On a scale of one to ten, where one is 'clear as mud' and ten is 'crystal clear,' how clear is our thinking about the actions we decided to take? It's useful to measure clarity in thinking before moving forward with a decision or action. Ask each leader to respond to the question with his or her own number along the scale. Then explore what's clear or not clear by asking follow-up questions.

One supervisor responds with "seven" on the scale of one to ten. Tom asks her what makes this a seven for her instead of a ten, to which the supervisor responds, "It's a seven for me because we have a few data points that help us focus our actions. We discussed it as a team, so we have more input than we would have if one of us tried to solve it alone. It won't take long for us to know if this solutions works."

After everyone had a chance to answer, Tom asked, **"What does a ten look like?"** This question reveals the best possible clarity–the ideal–when the problem is solved. The supervisors agreed that a ten is realized when the call center can meet customer needs, realize the efficiency standards for different customer needs, and customer service representatives have the training and skills to meet those needs. Everyone left the room with clarity, knowing what to do next.

Lead Like a Coach

Tom sat down and took a deep breath. He didn't have to solve the problem on his own. He decided to lead like a coach and ask some questions. He engaged his team and their best thinking that generated new insights, ideas, and actions. Great leaders ask questions and stay curious about the team's thinking.

Great leaders don't have all the right answers—great leaders ask all the right questions.

CHAPTER 14

Three Questions to Help You Hire the Best-Fit Employee

by Alonzo Johnson

Hiring best-fit employees has always been critical to organizational success. Changes in today's workforce have caused employers to focus more sharply on this critical task. Of course, there is no shortage of literature on the realities of the changing workforce landscape, but let's review it anyway.

As of January 2011, Baby Boomers (people born between 1946 and 1964) began turning 65 years old. Approximately 10,000 seasoned employees are reaching retirement age and exiting the workplace every day. According to the Pew Research Center, this trend is expected to continue until the year 2030. The exodus of Baby Boomers from the workplace will result in deficits in skills and experience that will challenge employers for decades.

Organizational leaders are keenly aware that effective hiring practices directly relate to the achievement of their goals. Effective hiring practices will result in a structured process for selecting best-fit employees who can replace retiring Baby Boomers and mitigate the risk of bankrupting their organizations of human capital.

A true test of an effective hiring process is how hiring managers make decisions about the best-fit candidates they choose to join their organizations. Many leaders who are tasked with making critical hiring decisions focus primarily on the candidate's experience and ability to do the job.

While the candidate's ability to do the job should be a key factor in the hiring decision, the candidate's motivation and fit for the culture are just as important. To find best-fit employees, leaders should devote equal amount of time to assessing each of the three areas during the hiring process. Leaders should seek answers to three main questions:

1. **Can the candidate do the job (the "Can")?** Does the can¬didate have the required skills, knowledge, education, and experience for this position? Is he or she able to articulate real experiences and information to demonstrate that he or she can do the job?
2. **Will the candidate do the job (the "Will")?** Is the candidate motivated to do the job? Are job requirements consistent with what the candidate enjoys doing? Do the career objectives of this per¬son align with the duties of the job, or are there advancement opportunities for him or her? Does the candidate's job history show the type of upward advancement you would expect of him or her?
3. **Is the candidate a good fit for the culture within the organization (the "Fit")?** Do the candidate's work behavior, style, and personality mesh with the job and the company? Will the candidate's level of assertiveness, stress tolerance, and interpersonal skills contribute to the team?

Answers to these questions will allow leaders to select best-fit employees who can hit the ground running and contribute to building the organization's future. Let's take a closer look at each of these questions.

Can the candidate do the job (the "Can")?

This is the obvious question that most hiring managers seek to answer. The hiring manager can seek answers to this question by gathering evidence about the candidate's knowledge, skills, and experience.

Knowledge and Skills Requirements

Knowledge and skills are not interchangeable; experience differentiates the two. For example, an administrative assistant can have "knowledge of" word processing and database management software, but it does not mean that he or she is effective at producing easy-to-read correspondences or building a database. It simply means that he or she knows the software. However, an experienced administrative assistant with knowledge of the software applications is likely to have the skills to be more effective at producing easy-to-read correspondences and building a database.

To further clarify my point, the following are actual examples, taken from ONET, of some of the top knowledge and skills requirements for an Admin Assistant. (We'll be using this position as an extended example for discussing your hiring needs.)

Knowledge

- *Clerical*—knowledge of word processing, managing records, transcribing, and designing forms.
- *English Language*—knowledge of English language including the meaning and spelling of words, rules of composition and style, and professional grammar.
- *Customer and Personal Service*—knowledge of principles and processes for providing customer and personal services.

Skills

- *Writing*—communicating effectively in writing to various audiences.
- *Active Listening*—giving full attention to what other people are saying, taking time to understand, appropriately asking and responding to questions.
- *Reading Comprehension*—fully comprehending written documents.
- *Speaking*—effectively conveying information through speech.
- *Time Management*—managing one's own time and the time of others.

As you can see from the above examples, knowledge and skills are not synonymous. When reviewing the job description to identify knowledge and skills requirements, make sure you examine the two terms independently.

Duties and Responsibilities

Now that you have determined what knowledge and skills the ideal candidate should possess, decide what he or she will actually do; these are otherwise known as duties and responsibilities. This decision will determine what role the employee will play in the organization. Following our previous example, the duties and responsibilities of an Administrative Assistant as identified by ONET include the following:

- Use computers for various applications, such as database management or word processing
- Answer telephones and give information to callers, take messages, or transfer calls to appropriate individuals
- Create, maintain, and enter information into databases
- Set up and manage paper or electronic filing systems, recording information, updating paperwork, or maintaining documents, such as attendance records, correspondence, or other material
- Operate office equipment, such as fax machines, copiers, or phone systems and arrange for repairs when equipment malfunctions
- Greet visitors or callers and handle their inquiries or direct them to the appropriate persons according to their needs
- Maintain scheduling and event calendars
- Complete forms in accordance with company procedures
- Schedule and confirm appointments for clients, customers, or supervisors
- Make copies of correspondence or other printed material

It is essential for you, as the hiring manager, to know the required duties and responsibilities of a job because they provide insight into the employee's role in the organization, and they will allow you to develop relevant interview questions that ultimately lead to hiring the best-fit candidate for the job.

Educational and Experience Prerequisites

Based on what you have decided are the important knowledge, skills, and duties for the position, which do you think is more important: education or work experience? Which makes a better employee?

Although this debate has circulated throughout the business world for a long time, there is not one conclusive answer. During my tenure as a staffing and development executive, even I could not conclusively answer this question. Almost every time I hired for a position reporting directly to me, my boss and I debated the importance of education versus experience for the job. When two candidates were equally qualified in all other areas, I usually selected the person with the most education rather than the person with the most experience.

My rationale was that my department developed and administered a number of specialized tools internally, including employee 360-degree assessments and employee engagement surveys. In the process, we used statistics to validate and analyze data. I needed people who understood statistics as well as I did or better.

But this is only one example of how you can weigh education and work experience when filling specific roles. Both are important; whether one seems more important than the other depends on the job. As the hiring manager, you should always weigh these factors carefully against the requirements of the job.

Will the candidate do the job (the "Will")?

Have you ever met an employee who possessed all the requisite skills, knowledge, and education, but who still was not considered a great employee?

In addition to gathering information about the candidate's competency level and ability to perform the job, you will also need to find out if the candidate is motivated to do the job.

Motivation

Motivation (the "Will") is an antecedent of job performance. This means that employees who are motivated to do a job will perform better than an employee who is not motivated. Based on Abraham Maslow's Hierarchy of Needs theory, people are motivated to satisfy certain lower-level needs first (things like food, water, shelter, and safety). Then, once those needs are satisfied, they will seek to satisfy mid-level needs (such as belonging and self-esteem). After those needs are met, they will pursue the need to become self-actualized. Self-actualization is the highest level of need to be satisfied. Person-organization fit seems to result in employees meeting both lower- and higher-level needs, which can lead to well-being and the achievement of self-actualization.

Candidates possess different motivating needs. The job and organizational requirements might not satisfy those needs. For example, the candidate might be motivated to join the organization because of the benefits that the organization offers. The organization might be looking for candidates with advancement potential. The organization's benefit structure might be less attractive to employees seeking to fulfill higher-level needs, so the candidate would not be motivated to advance in the organization.

Neither the candidate nor the organization benefits when there are mismatched motivating needs. The hiring manager should understand the needs of the job and the organization. During the interview, the hiring manager should gather information from the candidate to assess how well his or her needs match with the job and organizational requirements.

Review evidence from the interview to determine if the candidate is motivated to be a part of the organization and to perform the requirements of the job. For example, did the candidate present evidence during the interview that he or she conducted any research about the organization? Did you determine that the job was consistent with and supported the career goals of the candidate?

Is the candidate a good fit for the culture (the "Fit")?

Assessing candidate fit is like the third leg of the stool. To answer this question, the hiring manager will need to gather information about relevant work behaviors.

Relevant Work Behaviors

Often referred to as the "it factor" by some, work behaviors are characteristics individuals possess that are necessary for their success in organizations. It boils down to this: the "how" is just as important (if not more important) as the "what" in performing a job. Work behaviors can include characteristics such as assertiveness, independence, stress tolerance, interpersonal skills, or a specific personality trait. These intangible requirements can sometimes be difficult to identify when you are meeting someone for the first time, especially in an interview setting when the candidate is usually seeking to make a positive impression on the interviewer.

A candidate's work behaviors are a reflection of his or her values. When preparing to hire someone, be careful not to overlook work behavior requirements. Though otherwise qualified, a candidate who is lacking in these important requirements is not a good fit for the organization. Compared to a candidate with the required work behaviors, he or she is more likely to derail if hired.

Let's talk a little about what it means to derail.

Derailment occurs when an employee's career stalls because he or she has failed to perform as expected. Derailment often results in the employee exiting the organization, often involuntarily. I learned about derailment first-hand while working in corporate America; as the lead talent management executive, my boss asked me to determine why some employees derailed and left the company.

After reviewing the records of terminated employees, I was surprised to find that none of them derailed due to a lack of technical skills and competency (the knowledge and skills we just discussed); they all derailed due to a lack of one or more work behaviors. In this case, I found the lack of interpersonal skills and inability to work independently to be the primary reasons why employees derailed and left the company.

As a hiring manager, make sure you review the job at the beginning of the hiring process to determine how it will be required to function within your culture. Then, identify what "it factors," or work behaviors, are necessary for an employee to be successful in that role within your organization.

Hiring best-fit employees is and will continue to be one of the most important tasks that leaders perform to ensure the future success of their organizations. In light of the current Baby Boomers retirement trend, this task has become more critical. Answering the three questions discussed above allows hiring managers to focus on the "Can," the "Will," and the "Fit" for each candidate. This facilitates a holistic assessment of the candidate and yields better results to help hiring managers identify and select the best employee for the job and culture.

CHAPTER 15

Empathy and Ends-Based Communication:
You Haven't Said It If They Haven't Heard It!

by Joe DeSensi

Communication styles and message framing seem to be one of the largest hijackers of meetings and emails. From people working on the wrong priorities to the draining of emotional bank accounts, miscommunication is prevalent and often a needless waste of resources. It does not matter as much about what you say as it does what they hear. As the old joke goes, "what is said" and "what is heard" could get married because they are in no way related.

In the field of K-12 education, I often say, "You haven't taught it if they haven't learned it." To paraphrase for the world of communication, let me say it like this: "You haven't said it if they haven't heard it." This might sound silly at first, but the more you say this to yourself, the more empathetic and strategic your communication model will become.

In the chapter titled "A Lesson in Winning: How Are They Keeping Score?" I proposed that one has to understand what's important to others to be strategic about decision-making. Let me point the score-keeping arrow back at ourselves for the purposes of success in communication. Many times, people believe they have successfully communicated if *their* wording is sound, and they got *their* major points to the surface. Let's change the metric of success. You only get credit for communicating the things your audience understands and retains.

This fundamentally changes the game. We might have to use different media than we might normally want; maybe a face-to-face meeting would be better than a phone call. Even though we might have said everything we wanted to, we can't be sure that person retained the finer points of this mission-critical conversation. Ask yourself, for instance: are there important points, points you wanted to make sure people would retain, that you could have put into a handout or email prior to a meeting? Did you cover the items that needed to be covered, but without specifically talking about the actions people needed to take as a result?

Knowing only that I am upset about a project being behind is completely different from that same person understanding what exactly I want them to do next. We assume that, if others understand our premises, they will come to the same conclusions. Since people weigh issues differently and sometimes don't see the bigger picture, assuming someone will guess the conclusion of one's premises correctly is a communicator's problem, not a listener's problem.

If we judge by how much we say, we probably usually "win" the game of communication—our total volume of communication might be sufficient. However, if we then measure the action taken upon those critical messages over, say, the next quarter, we might have to admit that some of the shortcomings originate with the message not being properly understood and retained. Does the farmer judge success by how many seeds were dispersed, or by how many plants take root and produce? Does the teacher judge success by how many homework assignments they give or by how much the kids actually learn, remember, and prove on tests? It is the understanding of the broadcast, and not merely broadcasting that should drive leaders' communication strategies.

If we want to start judging ourselves more by results than speeches or emails, here are some best practices.

- **Own the process of the listener's understanding.** If a certain medium does not seem to work for certain messages, it is the communicator's problem if he or she keeps using it. If details are plentiful and specific, maybe they should be written down and the verbal message should only frame those details. Try this: instead of bringing everyone together for a two-hour meeting for important initiatives they'll be hearing for the first time, frame the meeting before they get there with as much information as you can give them. Have handouts and other materials with the key items that people need to understand, including any dates or deadlines that are particularly important. Send out a follow-up email with the specific responsibilities and action items each person should understand coming out of the meeting. Frame it, explain it, and explicitly communicate action items (remember that an action item = a unit of work + an owner or responsible party + a deadline).

- **Use checks for understanding.** Many times, communication is a one-way flow with a halfhearted "any questions?" or "does everyone understand?" at the end. Why not have your key personnel write a summary of how what you're saying impacts them and, specifically, what action items are now on their lists? For something important, it might be appropriate to have some sort of formalized check for understanding such as a form or questionnaire. Ask questions such as, "What is the most important thing I heard in the meeting today?" or "I need further information about the following..." or "My largest concern coming out today's meeting was..." or "What are some things that I need or need to know to make this initiative successful?" This may seem like a lot of overhead, so you might not want to do this for small or insignificant projects or initiatives—but if something is mission-critical or high-dollar-value, you can't afford not to have everyone clear from the beginning and working in the right direction.

- **Ask people how they like to get information.** Not everyone decodes the same way. It might be that some managers need to be able to ask clarifying questions on the spot while others need some time to digest details and then clear up ambiguities. We might not be able to accommodate every person every time, but based on the specifics of the message and the situation surrounding it, we can be strategic about what communication times and resources get us the most impact for our limited timeline.

- **Differentiation is the key to both communication and education.** Some people need a very detailed email or memo that they can refer to when they need to be refreshed about something. Others can't derive priorities or potential issues from a wordy email, and require Q&A to truly understand their roles and possible issues. You don't have to put every message in every format, every time. From your relationship with your team and the people with which are communicating, you will learn the most efficient ways to get the important things understood by the right people. If you are new to a team or group, it is better to err on the side of sending a message through a variety of formats rather than hoping you pick the right one; start with too much communication and optimize it, rather than giving too little information that requires recalibration and potential rework.

- **The more important something is, the more broadcasts and checks for understanding you should make.** If we have a big initiative, I might email some broad brush stokes before the big meeting, have some "meetings before the meeting" for the people who need them, have a well-run and professionally-facilitated meeting, send out minutes with action items, and ask key people to send me their understanding of what part they play and any questions or concerns their people might have. Always work backwards from what the success of a communication or an overall project looks like. The size of the initiative will help calibrate how much additional overhead you want to spend in double- and triple-checking the key parts.

One last note about your communication strategy: realize that communication on any given project or initiative blends with all of the other communication people get. For many people, emails all wind up in the same inbox; hardcopy memos might all be put in the same tray. One way to help people understand what is important is to *shield them from everything that is not.* If you send six emails a day to your whole team because certain thoughts hit you and you instantly turn around and communicate them, realize that not everyone will be able distinguish the important from the less important. Part of a good communication strategy is figuring out how to tamp down the noise that keeps people from identifying the key priorities. Efficiency of language, well-planned meetings with agendas and goals, routines and rituals for communications, and good processes for understanding checks are all part of making sure that people are hearing the important things that you are saying.

If we start with defining success as "the most people understanding the most important information in the most efficient formats" rather than "broadcasting things how we like to and hoping something sticks," our communication paradigm changes radically.

Lessons from the Classroom

This section takes lessons from the world of education and academia and applies the same core principles to the business world. Joe and Frank have recently written a book called *Turning Around Turnaround Schools: What to Do When Conventional Wisdom and Best Practice Aren't Enough.* Through the years, they have written in both the HOPE for Leaders newsletter and other Human Resource and leadership journals about the lessons business can learn from K-12 education.

Joe and Frank begin the section by introducing a new lexicon for evaluating and utilizing members of an organization or team in **"Do You Know Who's on Your Team Roster? You'd Better!"**

Next, in **"Embracing Business Lessons from the Rhythm of the Learner Year,"** they present an educational concept whose structure for students has parallels for how to evaluate and increase the potential of team members.

Joe and Frank then examine how toxic situations can be just as costly in the boardroom and the office as they are in classrooms in **"Combating Toxic Classrooms and Boardrooms."**

Joe and Frank explore how well-meaning managers and coworkers might actually be sabotaging the learning and potential self-sufficiency of employees by helping too quickly in **"Struggle Time versus the Well-Meaning Hero."**

Finally, they detail how to increase the quality of employees' work products by not allowing a comfort level with subpar work in **"Leading Out of the Comfort Zone to the Proficient Zone."**

CHAPTER 16

Do You Know Who's On Your Team Roster?
You'd Better!

by Frank DeSensi and Joe DeSensi

The roles your employees play on a team can affect every aspect of how you staff, how you lead, and how you plan the team's work. There are many ways to evaluate what personality types you have on a team and how they might work together. The purpose of this chapter is to develop a new approach to evaluating the membership and the power structures of a team.

Initiative Management Process

First, understanding your team is very important in change management or project management. Before looking at the makeup of a team, let's look at where you would perform this exercise. Classic project management theory includes five phases in a project or change management life cycle: initiation, planning, execution and monitoring, and closing the project.

Initiation, the first phase, unpacks the deliverables by explicitly detailing the line items that must be accomplished, then creating the project charter. Planning, the second phase, creates the actual game plan and is when most of the big picture, strategic work is done. The next two phases occur concurrently: the execution of the project plan and the monitoring of that execution to ensure it stays on track. The last phase, project closeout, institutionalizes the things that went well and mitigates issues for future projects by noting what didn't go well for future correction.

In a perfect world, you'd evaluate your roster of players right after the project charter was created—but that would assume you had good knowledge of the team members available to you. If you have no knowledge of your team, or have people assigned to you some time in after the project begins, this team member evaluation process could be ongoing throughout the execution of the project. Who is on your team, and how those members work individually and together, can have an impact on any of the following areas that deal with project planning and project execution: Impact on Charter or Plan, Project Scope, Responsibility Matrices, Work Breakdown Structures, Project Timeline, Resources Requirements and Allocation, Contingency Planning, and others.

Roster of Players

Many project managers already have a way to evaluate the team members' motivations or behavior preferences: Predictive Indexing, DISC, Myers-Briggs, and numerous other tools. These are great assessments, but in each case there are usually preconceived notions about certain letter combinations or personality curves. We offer a fresh way to assess the people on one's team by creating a new lexicon: The Roster of Players.

On the following page is a list of the team roles:

Roster of Players
KNOW YOUR TEAM

All Americans   Newbies

Cheerleaders   Keepers of the Old Flame

Lombardi Awards   Perpetually Overwhelmed

Grumblers   Naysayers

Procrastinators   Blockers and Saboteurs

The Roster

The 10 Roster Roles are split into 3 categories (Positive, Neutral, and Negative) and force-ranked within their categories.

POSITIVE	NEUTRAL	NEGATIVE
All-Americans	Newbies	Keepers of the Old Flame
Lombardi Award Winners		Perpetually Overwhelmed
Cheerleaders		Naysayers
Grumblers		Blockers and Saboteurs
Procrastinators		

Positive Roles

All-Americans—These are your go-to folks, your stars, your high-profile individuals that have very high yield. They might be your informal or *de facto* leaders when you're not there, and they might also be the ones that you groom in your succession planning to replace yourself should you be promoted or pursue other opportunities.

Strategies for All-Americans:
- Develop a shared vision, buy-in, and positive leadership with them.
- These are well-known, marquee players who should be placed in vital roles.

Lombardi Award Winners (LAWs)—LAWs are workhorses that do not need the high-profile role that is needed to satisfy All-Americans. They do not complain, they will do whatever needs to be done, and they are high-energy and high-yielding members with good attitudes and good work ethics. They can sometimes be groomed to be All-Americans with coaching in leadership skills and communication.

Strategies for Lombardi Award Winners:
- Help them focus on playing the game well.
- Hold them accountable for "game" accomplishments.

Cheerleaders—They are for whatever the leader is for. They rally support, communicate with a positive spin, and have a strong informal social network. They are not the best at completing complicated tasks and often need a heavy social component to their daily schedules. If harnessed correctly, they can be effective at communicating to the team and gaining support from some of the roles that usually have poor or negative attitudes.

Strategies for Cheerleaders:
- Provide shared vision and positive feedback for their extra efforts.
- Nurture them for informal leadership.

Grumblers—This group might sound like it should be in the negative column; true, they aren't as pleasant, but if managed properly, they can have the same work yield as LAWs. If you prefer, think of Grumblers as grumpy LAWs.

Strategies for Grumblers:
- Include them in the decision-making loop (sometimes they grumble because they don't have input or they don't understand the "why").
- Give positive feedback for successes.
- Set expectations for where and when grumbling will not be acceptable.

Procrastinators—This group has poor time management skills and little ability to estimate the time a task requires. They are normally fairly pleasant, but possibly less so as a looming deadline comes due. Still, they are a positive role.

Though requiring more oversight and strategic help, if properly managed they can yield a decent output.

Strategies for Procrastinators:
- Develop personal plans with timeline expectations.
- Establish regular visits and chats about progress to encourage movement.
- Chunk work into smaller portions can also help maximize their output.

Negative Roles
Keepers of the Old Flame—They are resistant to change. They remember a past that never was (meaning they romanticize or aren't sufficiently critical of the past). They can hijack meetings, work time, and productivity. Flame-keepers can be mid-yielding if managed well, but they are not good for onboarding newbies and can be dangerous if put in toxic social or functional groups.

Strategies for Flame-Keepers:
- Keep them focused on what can be, not what was.
- Gain their commitment to future vision, a personal plan, and accountability for implementation.
- Firmly intervene if stubbornly opposed to change.

Perpetually Overwhelmed—They always complain about being overworked. They have a priority list with 30 items tied for number 1. They can suffer from "analysis paralysis." They are similar to the Procrastinators, but have more issues with attitude and morale; think of them as under-producing grumblers. Like Flame-Keepers, the Perpetually Overwhelmed can be productive employees if managed, but they're not good for onboarding or in potentially toxic situations. They are sometimes mistaken for procrastinators, but it is important to distinguish because the two groups' strategies are different.

Strategies for the Perpetually Overwhelmed:
- Set priorities and hold accountable for reaching deadlines.
- Conduct regular "reality check" chats with leadership.
- Sometimes, they are so overwhelmed that they cannot get started with anything. Provide restarting or guidance.

Naysayers—Initially, they are always negative (or at least "concerned") about an issue. Their negativity comes more from resistance and fear of change than from actual strategic concerns. Change is an immediate negative to them, and only time and information can warm them to new initiatives. As with most of the negative roles, they should not be grouped in toxic work groups and are bad for onboarding newbies.

Strategies for Naysayers:
- Include in the planning loop whenever possible.

- Share new or bad information in advance or in a pre-meeting.
- Establish expectations for their piece of the new vision.
- Include in success celebrations.

Blockers and Saboteurs—This is the most insidious group because they are hard to spot. They can look like Cheerleaders or even All-Americans. The largest difference between this negative role and the others is that they do not wear their dysfunction on their sleeves and are not easily recognizable. The main characteristic of this group is that they attempt to seem positive or helpful, but they actively try to derail initiatives and undermine things behind the scenes that they may support publicly.

Strategies for Blockers and Saboteurs:
- There is usually little that can be done with this group because, once they're properly identified, they're difficult to trust.
- Immediately mitigate any power they have and double-check any plans for which they are in charge.
- Long-term, they usually need to go. We already have plenty of work dealing with people's skills, attitudes, and communication—we don't have time for those that harbor malicious intent.

Newbies are the swing role. They are new to your organization or new to your team. The die is not yet cast, so they have the greatest opportunity for increasing or decreasing potential work yield, energy, and attitude. What many leaders do when busy, or when at a critical point in an initiative, is to pair a newbie with a low-producing team member. Whether it's a naysayer who zaps the person's energy or a keeper of the flame who tells bleeding-heart stories of a past that never was, improperly onboarding a newbie is a mistake that costs many times its initial productivity savings in the future.

Strategies for Newbies:

- Pair a newbie with a Lombardi Award Winner or an All-American. Though it can lead to a short-term decline in that team member's work yield, it maximizes the potential of the newbie integrating well into the team and setting high goals for themselves from the beginning.
- Establish good habits and work expectations from day one.
- Give regular, specific, timely feedback.

Positive Roles at a Glance

ROLE	ENERGY	YIELD	DESCRIPTION
All-Americans	High	High	Go-to folks; interim leaders and marquee players
Lombardi Award Winners (LAWs)	High	High	Workhorses; people who get hard jobs done
Cheerleaders	High	Mid-Low	Ralliers; generators and sustainers of group energy
Grumblers	Mid	Mid	Grumpy workhorses; get jobs done with extra communication and hand-holding
Procrastinators	Mid	Mid-Low	Work-strategy-challenged; can get jobs done with extra assistance and supervision

Negative Roles at a Glance

ROLE	ENERGY	YIELD	DESCRIPTION
Keepers of the Old Flame	Mid	Mid-Low	Historians; can get moderate jobs done with extra framing and clear expectations
Perpetually Overwhelmed	Low	Mid-Low	Non-prioritizers; can get moderate jobs done with handholding or attitude adjustment
Naysayers	Low	Mid-Low	Low-priority, low-profile jobs
Blockers and Saboteurs	Any	Any	If their role doesn't quickly change, they do not get a role on your team

CHAPTER 17

Embracing Business Lessons from the Rhythm of the Learner Year

by Frank DeSensi and Joe DeSensi

As high-stakes testing and common core put more and more emphasis on using standardized test scores to hold schools accountable, it has become more important to quantify the return on every minute invested and every dollar invested in each student. One of the major problems that leaders have with current responses to problems is that they're focused mostly on content delivery and content volume. Schools are forced to use pacing guides, prepackaged lesson plans that don't adjust to the learner's needs, a schedule set up around adult and district needs, and assessments that test more than basic content retrieval. In other words, the actual needs of the student and the way in which the student will be evaluated are not necessarily the top criteria used for planning a school year.

The Issue

For many schools, their performance on state tests can be one of the most important metrics for deciding whether they require additional oversight for poor scores or, on the other hand, might get additional rewards and freedoms for better scores. If this is the case, then why are bus schedules, lunch schedules, school start and end times, school breaks, decisions on which teachers teach which classes, and the use of discretionary money all so far removed from the prime directive of schools? Why do none of those reflect the ultimate goal of making our students better learners and thinkers (which, as a byproduct, makes them more successful on state tests)?

What is the Rhythm of the Learner Year?

The authors of this chapter have an educational consulting company based in Louisville, Kentucky called Educational Directions (ED). ED has developed a learner-focused model called The Rhythm of the Learner Year. Amongst other factors for creating an entire school year focused on what most helps the student, they have split the school year into periods related to developmental needs of students at different points in the year, which helps raise the students' academic potential, helps students reach their potential, and finally, helps them to be successful on whatever "yardstick" tests districts and states have for measuring the progress of students and their schools.

The learner year is split into the following sections:

The Opening of School—This period begins two weeks before school starts and runs through the first three to five weeks of classes. In this period, the culture and expectations are explained and reinforced to the students as well as the administration. Educators' primary focus is enabling all students to be successful in their classes.

The Formative Period—This period begins after the opening of school and lasts until the winter break. During the Formative Period, diagnostics help educators understand where students are and where to increase their potential. In sports terms, this would be the equivalent of preseason strength training and studying the team's plays, techniques, and strategies. For educators, the focus in this period is on increasing student potential by building learning and performing skills.

The Calibrating Period—The Calibrating Period begins in January when students come back from winter break and continues until about three weeks before district or state testing begins. In the Calibrating Period, students must work at that new potential developed during the Formative Period. If work is turned in less than the level at which they will be tested, they must revise until acceptable. To continue with the sports analogy, this would be the regular season, where games are played and the score is kept exactly how it would be kept during the championship. The focus of the Calibrating Period is to enable all students to work to their potential.

The Testing Window—The Testing Window starts about three weeks before the actual testing cycle begins and ends when testing ends. This would be equivalent to the postseason and the championship. This is where abilities are assessed in a high-stakes format. The focus of the testing window is to maintain student motivation and effort and make sure that every student works to their potential throughout the assessment process.

The End of the Year (EOY)—EOY begins after testing and runs through the end of the school year. In sports, this would be any post-season time the team takes to institutionalize successes and find room for improvement in the future. The educator's focus is on introducing the expectations for next year's program and preparing students to make a successful transition to the next level.

How the Rhythm of the Learner Year is Used in Education and Business

With this process, ED creates an environment in which the students can be successful, diagnosis where the students are individually and then works on the potential of those students, raises the students' work to that new potential, creates a best-case scenario for the students being tested on what they have learned and how they think, and finally helps them process that year's learnings and look ahead to their next year and next assessments.

With this understanding of on-boarding and developing a student, how can these same principles be applied to the business world? Let's start by looking at the same kinds of questions we should be asking in our companies:

- Are we onboarding employees and kicking off new initiatives and projects in a way that starts by creating a successful environment that will harness the best of what every employee can offer?
- Are we taking employees that have untapped potential and giving them the coaching or professional development they need to produce at a higher level and rise as high as their abilities might take them?
- When we develop employees and invest (time, money, and effort) into new or enhanced skill sets, are there opportunities for them to then use those skills and escape their comfort zone without fear of failure keeping them from trying something different?
- Are we being clear about what business success and individual success look like, and are we tracking the right metrics that support the type of employee we are trying to groom?
- Finally, are we institutionalizing what we learn and harnessing all the best practices we can to actively groom our culture, all the way down to details like a deliberate onboarding process?

What if we applied The Rhythm of the Learner Year to businesses and used it to focus culture, employee development, work cycles, communication processes, promotion, and leadership around what truly helps employees work well?

As in the case of the school system, first start by looking at the official (and unofficial) rules, including standard operating procedures, Human Resources policies and procedures, compensation and bonus plans, onboarding processes, dress codes, workplace flexibility, work-from-home availability, leadership and professional development, and any other "rituals and traditions" a business might have. If you were to design the workplace you wanted from scratch, how many of these factors would you consider and how many would you omit?

Shirley Jackson has a classic American short story called "The Lottery." A very short synopsis of the story is that at a harvest festival in the 1800s, a group of people are slowly going through a selection process, and as they do, they talk about how they can't remember exactly how the lottery started or why they are doing it, but they can't believe some neighboring towns no longer have such an event. At the very end of the short story, it turns out that they are selecting a person to be a harvest sacrifice—even though no one can remember exactly why the sacrifice takes place. This story is a quintessential cautionary tale about remembering why rules were originally developed.

I mention that story for a reason. Suppose, for example, that at a given company no one is allowed to take vacation time in the month of June one year, simply because of a project or production schedule in progress. Years later, that project or product line may no longer be active, but everybody expects not to be able to take vacation in June, and new people may "fall in" with the "rule" even though the reason for the rule has long since disappeared.

"Opening School" for Business

Onboarding an employee or group of employees can be very similar to starting a new school year. There is a new leader, norms and culture are being established, expectations aren't yet clear, and there is certain wariness on the part of the newbies. ED has a saying that you cannot win the school year in the first three weeks, but you can lose the school year in the first three weeks. If the school year starts poorly, without discipline in place and expectations of success being set and reinforced at every turn, the whole fall semester can be lost just trying to restore order in the school. An inefficient and poorly-run opening of school can doom an entire school year and testing cycle.

Similarly, we cannot create a great employee who understands everything that is expected of them in terms of work, success, and performance, much less who is motivated for new projects, in the first few weeks—but, if we're not careful, we can disenfranchise that new employee during the onboarding process in ways that can take years to undo (or, more likely, shorten that employee's tenure with you). When a team is really busy and they have some new recruits, normally the recruits are either given busy work until someone can work with them, or they're placed with some of the least productive people to make sure that the high-energy, high-production people are left undiminished. Think about the logic in this: we are either (A) telling the recruits that they're not important because they can't produce yet, or, even worse, (B) we put the recruits with the people we would least like for them to emulate.

The onboarding process should envision what a great, successful employee (given the proper start) would look like over the next three to four years, and every action and policy should support grooming the employee to that end. We should pair new employees with the best of the department or company, and they should have regular interaction with supervisors and coaches giving them specific, timely feedback to make sure that they don't develop a comfort level of working below leadership's expectations. The more deliberate and employee-focused this process, the quicker green employees become seasoned professionals in terms of both work product and cultural fit.

Using The Formative Period to Increase Production and Worker Potential
Once an employee has been on-boarded and is starting to produce, the Formative Period might cover the first four months to two years of the position, and in this time leadership both capitalizes on current strengths and identifies the ways that the employee needs to develop next. This could be formal; you could use performance improvement plans to let employees know exactly where you want to see progress and explain the specific activities and expectations surrounding those areas.

As an example: if a person is a poor communicator, Toastmasters or Dale Carnegie classes might be part of the prescription. If a person produces well but doesn't play well with the team, a 360 evaluation followed by external coaching might be a way to take a good employee and make them a great coworker as well. If there are technical hurdles to leap, certification classes or pairing with an expert for mentoring might fill out the suite of competencies a person needs. These plans have to be specific, timely, individualized for the person, well-communicated, and constantly monitored and adjusted.

We must always start with Hippocrates' adage: "Do no harm." If something is tough but slowly getting the results that we need, we push on. If a process is disenfranchising employees, or there doesn't seem to be any benefit coming from the time and money spent, stop and figure out a new plan.

Rarely will we get a person that has a complete skill set and that is perfectly suited for a new work environment. Sure, we could take what we get, including competency deficiencies or social and morale issues, and choose not to deal with those shortcomings because we don't see the return on investment. If that doesn't sound good, then we need to develop an ideal of what an excellent employee looks like; through onboarding and managing, we need to figure out the strengths and weaknesses of each new employee; then, we need to develop a personalized action plan to bridge the gap between the current state and the ideal state of that specific person. Not every person can become the ideal, no matter how much time and effort is invested—but, conversely, very few people lack potential for movement if they'd be developed in the right way.

Leveraging the Calibrating Period for Bigger and Better Business Ventures
There is only so much one can learn in the classroom or under the wing of a mentor. At some point, the culture must require us to get out, try, possibly fail, learn, and get better. Not unlike the "helicopter parents" that have created issues for some of the Millennial generation, constant oversight and help can actually hinder the learning and doing processes. People learn more from their

own mistakes, especially when they can discover the answers or better path on their own.

In schools, the Calibrating Period is used to make sure students are reaching their full potential. Where in the Formative Period students are working on individual skills that will make them self-initiated learners, they do not necessarily have to show mastery of every skill yet. In the Calibrating Period, work turned in below the test's level is returned to the student to revise until proficient. Revision to proficiency helps students learn and gives them the ability to self-assess where—and why—their work is less than acceptable. After several iterative cycles of revising subpar work to standards, a student will slowly learn to build that value into the initial draft. "First attempts" made later in the Calibrating Period should look like third or fourth attempts from the beginning of the period.

In business, leaders need to define what success looks like, then let employees take a crack at attempting a project or deliverable. Afterwards, review both the exemplary parts and the deficiencies, then have a dialogue about what is needed to get the work up to an acceptable standard. Sometimes this can take three, four, or more iterations and might seem like a waste of time if the leaders could just fix it themselves and be done with it. The problem is that substandard work and reliance upon the leader for all of the hard thinking and completion work will remain as they are until the capacity for better work is built into the employee. The longer leaders accept substandard work, the harder it is to require improvement on that work, since the employee had consistently been shown that their work was acceptable.

Both students and employees don't just need to exhibit specific traits or behaviors; they need to be able to do the thinking work and approach learning and its tests systemically. We are not just imparting content to students; we are teaching them to think about that content and how to manipulate and translate those ideas into something else. Similarly, we don't just want to teach employees an exact process for an exact set of inputs; we want them to understand what success looks like at the end and the many paths one can take to get there, which may sometimes include creating a new path. Innovation requires an understanding of the big picture; employees that have no understanding of context or border processes between their work and "The Work" will only be drones relying heavily on a leader's instruction.

The Testing Window and How Businesses Judge Success

In K-12 education, the rubric for judging a school is usually pretty clear. Depending on the state or school district, there is usually an algorithm that takes into account school grade and metrics such as graduation rate, absenteeism, conduct issues, college readiness, and others, which feed into an overall school grade. On top of that, there are common-sense factors such as crime, bullying, bad news stories, community reputation, and other factors that weigh in on a school's level of success.

Sometimes, in business, success can be a little harder to define. There is the success of the company, the success of the individual department or business unit, and the success of the individual member, as well as different groups or verticals that sometimes get lumped together. A person could have a banner year—for instance, a salesperson meeting 130% of his or her sales numbers—while the company struggled. It could be that the company had a great year, as did a person's department, but either through work product or cultural fit, a person might not do well based on the manager's metrics of success.

Similar to the vision and the mission of the company, business units should be nested in the goals of the whole company, department goals should be nested inside of the goals of their business units or divisions, and individual performance plans and individual goals should be nested inside of the metrics of success of their departments.

Employees must know comprehensively what success looks like and how they are being judged. Also, they need to understand how their part feeds into the larger picture of success. Many compensation plans and bonus structures don't necessarily support what the company claims success looks like. Companies say that they value teamwork, but they give bonuses based on individual performance. They say that they are trying to build a great place to work, but there is no metric to measure how coworkers interact and are perceived by each other. Quality is considered hugely important, but bonuses are often given purely on profit margin.

The problem is not that we grade on one thing but actually want another. The problem is that we want both things, but we only use one as a metric. If the company wants to pilot new products, they can't be surprised if their sales team (who is judged only by gross sales) mostly pursues existing channels with the products they're most comfortable selling. If a project manager is only judged by on-time delivery and delays, we can't be completely surprised if they get rude or even unprofessional with anyone delaying their critical path.

Step one is making sure that the things important to overall success are the things actually being tracked and incentivized. Step two is making sure everybody understands what is important, what success looks like, what is not acceptable, what the rewards are for success, and finally, what the penalties are for failure. (Failure meaning that an important metric was not met, not that someone tried something new but it did not work out. Failed attempts at innovation are good for learning and breakthroughs. Failure on the things the company considers most important is an unacceptable type of failure).

End of the School Year and Closing Out a Project Cycle or Fiscal Year

In a school year, the time after the testing window until the end of school should not be something you set aside for field trips and field days. The way most American school districts work, we take a long break in the summer (a carryover from more agrarian times). Many times, the opening weeks of school in the subsequent year are for reviewing material from the previous year that was taught but forgotten. There are activities and strategies schools can use to pack away those learnings at the end of the year that make them more easily retrievable at the beginning of the subsequent year. Students doing meaningful work that translates and makes personal significance out of the year's learnings puts those learnings into long-term memory, where it can survive a hot summer of fun in the sun. Closing out a school year with the next year already in mind really allows the next learning cycle to start as soon as the current testing window ends.

In business, at the end of a project or the end of a calendar or fiscal year, how do we deconstruct what went right and what went wrong, and how do we institutionalize the good and mitigate the bad? This should be built into the fabric of the project lifecycle for the business year. Formal processes, meetings, postmortem reports, and processes for institutionalizing lessons learned should be part of every department's best practices. Even if we stumbled onto an answer by luck, let's make sure we have it at our fingertips the next time the same issue arises. If we make some assumptions and things go horribly awry, the only true failure would be to not capture the learnings and find ourselves in the same situation again.

Adding the good ideas and processes to a proverbial toolbox, doing a root-cause analysis of sub-optimal results, and capturing the prescriptive ideas while they're still fresh is the only way to create a culture of continuous improvement. Institutional knowledge and a learning culture must be something specifically groomed and supported to last. Without constantly trying to be better tomorrow than we are today and building our metrics and processes around that idea, we become unintentional and unpredictable in terms of future results.

Final Note

In schools, the ability of students to use the knowledge they have learned in a meaningful way (as assessed by testing mechanism) is the largest component of how the school is graded. Anything that supports that ability should be weighted heavily, and the things that don't support (or sometimes even diminish) that ability should be seen as lesser priorities. In business, we need to define what success looks like for a company with a charter that defines comprehensive goals for "winning." The things that inhibit overall success—or an individual's eventual contribution of their full potential to that success— should be addressed and mitigated.

If we base our business practices on what makes happy, productive, confident employees work to their highest level and participate in all levels of success, we will develop a culture of innovation and learning that will retain great employees and attract the best and the brightest.

CHAPTER 18

Combating Toxic Classrooms and Boardrooms

by Frank DeSensi and Joe DeSensi

Many of the same dynamics exist in both schools and the workplace. Politics, social dynamics, and power struggles all play out in high schools, middle schools, and elementary schools just as they do in many places of business. Maybe then, some of the same remedies that have proved helpful in the halls of academia can cure what ails us at work.

In education, we struggle with toxic environments. Schools and classrooms can sometimes develop an environment that is anti-learning and actually prohibits performance improvement. When this happens, the institutional culture, climate, and social structure work to prevent meaningful learning for students and meaningful lessons for teachers. This derails students and teachers (and if bad enough, school leaders) and can impact surrounding classes for weeks. It can also create a channel for students who experience a toxic culture to carry it with them to other schools and, ultimately, into society.

The causes of a toxic environment are many and varied. On one hand, the environment may have adult causes: for example, internal power struggles, or clashing reactions to change can cause the climate among educators to break down and drain the performance of people involved, affecting everyone around them. Stressful situations, contract disputes, mandated changes, or professional jealousies can have the same effect.

On the other hand, issues can also develop at the student level. Interpersonal issues between key students, power struggles between teachers and students, a weak teacher or a substitute teacher with poor classroom management skills, or other barriers like outside interruptions or frequent diversions can undermine a sound classroom culture and create a toxic environment.

In the K-12 education arena, testing results have become high-stakes. Students must be caught up if they are behind; they need to be taught at least one year's worth of content in a given school year and possibly more if they have fallen behind; they must be able to demonstrate their knowledge in the manner in which they will be assessed; schools and individual students' progress must be tracked so the few discretionary resources that exist can be targeted to the right areas. A toxic environment makes all of these tasks difficult, if not impossible.

In addition to the inefficiencies associated with toxic environments, there is a huge cost to the school's "bottom line." A toxic school or classroom disrupts not only the learning of each student in the class, but negatively impacts all of the other students in the classes those students have for the rest of the day. It can also carry over in the teachers' other classes, resulting in reduced energy or effectiveness there (multiplied then by the number of classes left in the day and the number of students in each class). The ripples spread and multiply quickly, and schools begin to fail at their most essential job: teaching.

In business, a similar situation can exist: the toxic leader can cause a good team to underperform; the toxic team member who hijacks meetings and deflates the sails of his or her cohort can create an environment in which cooperative work is impossible; the toxic committee that (for some reason) meets first thing in the morning and zaps all of the participants can reduce both effort and quality of output from everyone in attendance.

In schools, it is said that if a school leader knows that a teacher cannot teach a student (especially if it is in a tested area), and there is another option available, then it is no longer a teaching issue. It is a leadership issue. If you have dysfunctional teams or groups under your domain and you allow them to remain intact, it is not subordinate issue; it is a leadership issue. Sometimes issues are not addressed because it is not perceived they have hit a tipping point to be something that needs to be addressed. When this occurs, like a toxic class, a toxic workplace has a huge cost associated with it which is a de-motivated and disengaged workforce that is not committed to helping achieve the organization's goals.

CHAPTER 19

Struggle Time versus the Well-Meaning Hero

by Frank DeSensi and Joe DeSensi

Being a fan of superheroes and action movies, we (like so many others) often feel an instinct that swooping in and saving the day is always the right thing to do. In schools, compassionate teachers rush to the aid of students failing to grasp the task at hand, and from an altruistic perspective, they are doing "good" work. Unfortunately, from an educational perspective, they are often preventing children from the opportunity to discover something for themselves, which would both strengthen the child's problem-solving skills and store the learning in the child's long-term memory.

The concept of "struggle time" is counterintuitive to the Well-Meaning Hero that wants to clear the path and make something less of a struggle. As an example, think of someone undergoing physical rehabilitation; if you've ever been through such treatment, you know that someone does not go to rehab for things to be easy. Rehab trains damaged muscles, in incremental steps, to do more and more over time; if one never taxes his or her muscles, the muscles don't get any stronger. If the doctors or therapists required only what the patient could do without struggle, they'd have told the patient to stay in bed; they require struggle because it's the only way for the patient to return to health.

Likewise, if students aren't allowed to struggle at the beginning of a task, or organize their thoughts and create an initial approach, what they learn will not be as permanent and they will become teacher-dependent for their learning.

Also, when students work only in their comfort zone, the depths to which they learn something will be limited; in most cases, only new content will be learned, rather than process, or how to initiate one's own learning. Much of learning is the question of how to learn, as much as the specific content being covered at any given moment. Proverbially speaking, "struggle time" teaches students to fish. The Well-Meaning Hero does the heavy lifting for the students, which only helps them in that moment—if you will, giving them a fish instead.

As leaders in business, are we training our people to fish for themselves? How often do we assign a task or project and immediately receive questions about how to start or what to prioritize? If the task and outcomes are clear, we should allow our people to struggle to develop a plan, and then give them help if they get off track or hit a road block. By doing this, we develop an independent workforce that can innovate and work competently with less oversight.

If projects cannot begin until we do the initial heavy lifting, then there is a much smaller cap on how many projects we can manage as leaders. It also means that we are creating a comfort zone that is dependent on our presence and involvement. This is guaranteed to limit the innovations we can create as a team, rather than harness the creativity and experience of everyone in the group. With the right praise and instilled confidence, a team can produce more, challenge employees to do heavier lifting, and allow leadership to facilitate and mentor rather than being the workflow bottleneck and the only source of new ideas.
If one begins with the end in mind, surely he or she wants to maximize the potential of his or her team. If employees are not allowed to struggle, take risks in a safe environment, and then be guided and mentored by a supportive leader, maximum potential will not be achieved. The Well-Meaning Hero steals development opportunities in order to make single moments easier. The wise leader knows that allowing workers to struggle and grow increases capacity and often job satisfaction as well.

This may force the business leader to step outside of his or her traditional leadership role. Many ad hoc workgroups will need to be trained in brainstorming, task analysis, tactical and logistical planning, and effective teamwork. In addition, the leader will have to develop in students a perception of what a proficient outcome would be and also what expectations are for proficient work needed to produce the outcome. This understanding will become an important part of the group culture.

The leader will also have to take the time to initiate, monitor, and tweak the group culture and climate so that all participants can feel valued and can be productive. Rituals, routines, and expectations will have to be established to further an effective group work. Only by developing this culture can the leader be sure that the group operates at or above its potential, reaches the goals set for themselves, and raises performance for the whole business.

A leader must also be able to facilitate the group's work. Resources, time, and expertise may be needed for the group to reach and grow its potential. It's important to note, though, that while the leader can help shape culture, broker resources, and facilitate planning, it is important that the group be allowed to function as a working group. The group will need to struggle and grow, to develop its own approach to the task at hand, evaluate its progress, and make adjustments to its processes, procedures, rituals and routines. It will be this struggling with the task that enables the group to grow to the task rather than the leader's direction.

CHAPTER 20

Leading Out of the Comfort Zone to the Proficient Zone

by Frank DeSensi and Joe DeSensi

As a companion piece to the "Struggle Time" chapter, we want to better introduce the idea of Revision to Proficiency. In Struggle Time, an educator lets a student have time to organize their thoughts, visualize the assignment, and self-initiate the learning process. Revision to Proficiency is the other bookend of this process.

In Struggle Time, the teacher wants a student to "try." Once an initial work product is turned in, a teacher wants the student to make one or more attempts to transform the first draft into something that would be considered proficient. This is a critical point. If a teacher allows someone to struggle through a task, and either the process or the product fails to meet expectations, then it's important that the teacher require (and assist if necessary) the student's reworking the product to make it proficient. This creates a perception of what proficient work and proficient products look like. Without revision to proficiency, the person who produces substandard products, or performs tasks in a less-than-proficient manner, can develop a comfort zone around below-level performance. In a high-stakes accountability classroom, this is a disaster for the student and the student's test scores. In an organization, it's a disaster for the business's bottom line.

Businesses use some of the same short-term "Band-Aid" techniques used by teachers in the classroom. If an employee turned something in, we will fix it after the fact and rarely give the employee the feedback that would help them produce better work next time—never mind actually working with them to revise it. Leaders don't skip this to keep the employee at a lower level of ability; almost always, it's simply a time issue where they just don't see themselves having the time to do anything other than quickly polish the work, pass it on, and move on to the next fire on their list.

This can create real issues in terms of building capacity, raising employee expectations or responsibilities, blindsiding employees during performance reviews, and generally setting a consistent tone for what good work looks like on the team. By no direct intent, leaders gradually train their employees to underperform and, at the same time, make the employees feel like they are doing sufficient work.

The same way Struggle Time is important to how employees initiate or approach work, Revision to Proficiency teaches employees how to successfully finish an initiative. Think about this: if you had to turn in a report every week, something you filled out to the best of your ability, and you never got any feedback, wouldn't you be shocked to eventually learn that you had been doing the report wrong for an entire year? Your response would probably be something to the effect of, "Well, if you'd just told me, I could've done this the way you wanted me to."

With that empathetic mindset, let's put ourselves on the other side of the equation. Can you really be upset with someone that has a bad ongoing work behavior if you neither tell the person they were working below standards nor take the time to show them examples of proficient work to help them with their own?

It is a leader's job to help employees understand what good work and good behavior looks like around the office, and then to incrementally help the person get there. Here are some guidelines for helping "students" revise their first pass into something stellar:

- **Don't accept mediocre work as a finished product.** If students are working below the level at which they will be assessed and more is not asked of them, teachers can train students to produce work below their potential and below their expectations from the district and state. If an employee is turning something in that is less than you were expecting, likewise, you must define the level at which they should be working and give them opportunities to fix what they have done, or they will continue to operate below expectations. Mere feedback is usually not enough; let them take that "unfinished" work product and add value to it. If it is still below the minimum level required, be specific with where it needs more attention and let them try again. Building proficiency in one's employees and teammates produces huge dividends; work starts to be complete from the first submission, rather than requiring time and effort for rework.

- **Show what proficient work looks like, but don't communicate an exact path.** It is unfair to ask students to create a good product without defining or demonstrating what good work looks like. Also, the teacher should not do all the thinking on how to improve an assignment; after all, teachers will not be able to do the hard thinking for students on a state or college prep test. It's right for the teacher to show what proficient work looks like and let students think, but it's wrong for the teacher to do all the thinking about how to get work from its current state to its desired state. In the same way that Struggle Time helps students raise problem-solving skills and higher levels of engagement with a particular project or initiative, Revising to Proficiency helps tap into some of those same skill sets to take a work in progress and add the value needed to make it truly complete. If the exact path for fixing something is given to them, then they will only be able to fix products that have the exact same deficits. By talking through what the finished product looks like and letting them struggle with what needs to be done, the student or employee builds tactics and brain patterns that will help them with the "approach" to this sort of problem, rather than just the solution for this particular problem.

- **Reward genuine efforts.** Revision to Proficiency is about process, not content. The final product is not as important as the approach, the persistence, and the process of adding value to each revision. This is not an easy skill, and praise and rewards go a long way to building confidence. The "win" is in getting a student to put forth the effort. In revising, it may take a few attempts for someone to figure out how to get from where they are to where you say they need to be, so how they approach those revisions is what you want to be rewarding. If they are taking your feedback and making a concerted effort to produce what you have defined, there is a genuine victory here even if they fall short. If effort is meaningful, thoughtful, and shows a genuine attempt to meet the standards that you have set, then the person is on their way to self-sufficiency. It takes some frontloading of effort, but again, it pays dividends over time.

- **Do a Process Closeout.** After the final version of the work is completed, have the student verbalize his or her approach and what techniques they used, whether in speech or writing. This translating activity allows the students to be more introspective on their own processes, and it puts the process into long-term memory so it can be more easily retrieved when needed in the future. What questions did they ask? Do they need help from anyone, or more information? Did they make any assumptions that were wrong? If they were going to start the process on this particular item again, how would their approach be different than last time? Standardizing an approach for how one discovers their target product and defines the processes they use to keep themselves on track is the ultimate goal of the revision process.

For a leader striving to develop a self-initiated team that prizes innovation, all these principles have direct application to the business world. As was the case with Struggle Time, a leader wants employees to be able to self-start and develop creative approaches to complex tasks; that leader wants employees to be able to take something and add value to it. A self-initiated workforce that can kickstart complex initiatives and add value to work products will pay dividends in output, in employee engagement, and in keeping leadership working at a strategic level.

Pearls from Entertainment

This category is the authors' favorite. These come about because, at one point, we had a series in the HOPE for Leaders newsletter of short capsules called "Pearls from the Cinema." In combing through five years of the articles, we also found plays and television shows that we used for extended metaphors for leadership education. All of the chapters in this section pull from different types of popular media and distill lessons that are sometimes easier to consume with familiar examples like these.

Hope and Joe discuss the usefulness of empathy as taught by a con man in **"Empathize Like a Maverick."**

Joe and Susan unpack the idea of "encoding" and "decoding" the messages sent between people—including what we do wrong and how we can do better—in **"Decoding *The Imitation Game.*"**

Joe and Susan present an unexpected metaphor for reading people more effectively in **"Reading People with The Simpsons' Australian Toilet Premise."**

Joe and Susan examine how assumptions can create a false reality in **"A Lesson in Assuming from *The Usual Suspects.*"**

Finally, Hope closes out the section (and the book) with inspirational lessons from Thornton Wilder's Our Town in **"*Our Town*: Lessons for LEADing Your Life."**

CHAPTER 21

Empathize Like a Maverick

by Joe DeSensi and Hope Zoeller

Over the last several years, we have written several articles and book chapters about empathy—why it is important, how it helps make more strategic and cost-effective decisions, and how it aids in retaining your best employees and motivating your work force. Empathy is not simply feeling sorry for someone when something bad happens to them or wishing them the best when something good happens. Empathy is being able to project into the way a person thinks that helps explain why things make a person happy or sad; it is getting into the head of an audience, and thinking the way they think.

One of the best ways to use empathy as a strategic tool is to become a better listener. Take time to listen and probe, but not in a way where you frame the conversation. Use short open-ended questions and see where the person takes the conversations. Do not focus on "gathering content"; instead, focus on processing information with context and understanding the sender.

A great example of this can be found in the movie *Maverick* starring Mel Gibson, based on the TV series of the same name. Bret Maverick was a gambler and a bit of a con man. In the movie, he asks to sit in on a poker game. After some initial reluctance by the other players, he suggests that he will probably lose every hand for an hour. They allow him to join, and he proceeds to intentionally lose for an hour. After the hour is up, he begins winning—a lot. He is accused of cheating, so he reveals his strategy. He might have lost every hand the first hour, but he was "researching" how the other people played the game. He looked for tells, styles, strategies, and other clues. After doing his research, he was able to play each hand with a lot more insight than if he had played on level footing from the beginning.

The key for Maverick wasn't knowing whether the players were good at poker, nor whether or not they were lucky. It also wasn't his intention to burn an hour only to "re-enter" the game and win on his raw strength or skill as a card player. His strength came from understanding how people make their decisions, how they communicate their strengths and weaknesses, how they react as good things and bad things happen to them, and finally how to create the circumstances to drive them towards the actions he wanted them to want to take. Once someone knows the "algorithm" of a game, there is very little left at the mercy of chance. Once Maverick's hour was up, the rest of the players never stood a chance simply because none of them were approaching the game in the same way.

So—without sending everyone out to find the nearest gambling tables—what lessons can we learn from Bret Maverick?

1. **Sit back and watch folks.** In the book *Five Dysfunctions of a Team*, the new CEO waits on making any changes to the company and doesn't even lead her own meetings until after having spent a couple weeks gathering information. It's true that sometimes you can't wait, and you have to make immediate decisions with very little contextual information; in those cases, you play the numbers based on business best practices and let the chips fall where they may. If you have the time to not make an immediate decision, don't make one. See how the natural order of things seems to work, view it as a spectator, and see as much of the reality of the situation with which you're being presented, especially the people within it. The more data-driven and contextual your prescription, the

more likely you are to target the root cause of an issue, or perhaps greatly reduce the amount of time a remedy might take.

2. **Let your people talk.** If you want to know how your people think, give them opportunities to do most of the talking. If there is an issue, call them in, ask some open-ended questions, and keep quiet. If the purpose is to gather content on an issue, you might have to be specific on initial questions and follow-ups. If the key is to understand process, the initial questions are just a chance to open up the black box and see what's working inside. The content is almost irrelevant beyond it being pertinent and timely enough to really get people thinking. The more open-ended questions will give more insight into the whole of how things work in a broader context from more thorough description, rather than just a series of little data points from answering a series of narrow, closed questions.

3. **Win the war, not the battle.** I have worked for leaders who need to own the outcome of every discussion. If they already have a plan, they will skip the inquiry of ideas and dictate an outcome, whether they have the hearts and minds of their people or not. By having some discussions that others dominate and by seeking ideas first rather than always using a top-down, dictatorial approach, you might find people coming to some of the same conclusions and therefore having some ownership in the final idea. You might also find that they're able to fill out the idea you have in mind. As the old saying goes, "One of us is not as strong as all of us." In our case, we should say that, "None of us knows as much as all of us." Embracing this idea alone can help build a culture of inquiry and an empathetic understanding of how key people think and work.

4. Similar to #3, for larger issues and non-crisis projects, **it is cheaper to lead than to manage.** The difference between leadership and management is not the outcome, but rather the overall cost of that outcome. Managers can get people to do what they want, but leaders can get people to want to do what they want. If you can motivate people to do their best rather than manage them into a state of compliance, you get more production for the same cost over a period of time. More effort towards

good, strong leadership at the top gets a good return on investment as it trickles through the ranks. Empathizing like a Maverick gives a person the ability to communicate with the precision of a rifle rather than the broad scatter of a shotgun because the message is specifically packaged for the receiver. Instead of going to general management trends or loose understandings of how key personnel work, it is slowly refining a targeted strategy to efficiently communicate and motivate the individual or the specific group.

Empathetic understanding is access to an information set that can then be used in strategic planning. Empathy doesn't have to mean hugging trees or singing "Kumbaya." Quite the opposite: it can be a way to both maximize the return on investment of rewards and incentives and mitigate bad news or demotivating factors.

You have to make decisions in the "world that is" rather than "the world you wish were." To this end, empathy goes a long way. It takes patience and real effort, but it is a skill set and a process that will pay dividends over time. So stop managing and start listening, and empathize like a Maverick.

CHAPTER 22

Decoding *The Imitation Game*

by Joe DeSensi and Susan Draus

Every day, each and every one of us speaks in code. "Speaking in code," while a helpful plot device in movies, is not conducive to efficient and effective communication in the workplace. There is a significant difference between *sender-based communication* (where we communicate in the same manner that we think, basing our messages directly upon our thoughts) and *ends-based communication* (where we work backwards from how our receivers will understand the message and then tailor that message to convey as much as possible).

Most people tend to speak in a sender-based fashion. It's easier to compose this way, but again, we all speak in code; sender-based communications requires a cipher to understand. Despite the glaring pitfalls with this type of communication, most people use it because they can send the same message ten different times without having to account for any differences among the listeners. However, this also leaves room for ten different interpretations of the original message!

In order to create an end-based communication, we have to know something about the listeners we are intending to reach. As a sender, you must know how the receivers think and what is important to them to know how to create an ends-based message (which requires empathy to some degree). This level of sophistication in crafting a message may take more time initially, but the end result is clearly superior. With ends-based communication, you have created a message that has the sole purpose of being understood by the receiver, a message with no ambiguity in desire or intent.

There is an amazing movie, set during World War II, called *The Imitation Game*. The movie tells the story of how Alan Turing decrypted the Germans' Enigma code that was integral to many of the early German successes in the war. Until Turing's successes, the Enigma code was thought unbreakable. The Allies had been intercepting German communications for a long time, but because of the Enigma code, the Allies couldn't understand the content of the communications. That's to say: the sender-based communication was gibberish to one of its (unintended) recipients, in this case the Allies, and that was entirely the point of the Enigma code to the Germans: the Allies could not make use of these intercepted messages and, as a result, the war continued in the Germans' favor, with thousands of Allied casualties hanging in the balance.

The Enigma decryption machine was a complex cipher for Turing to build. He had to define the likely perimeters of the German Army's communication protocols and understand how these transmissions were encrypted in order to decrypt the messages with any accuracy and expediency. Without this understanding, the Allies' interceptions were useless. In a sense, Turing was doing the most difficult version imaginable of what we try to do every day: understand what other people are saying by "decrypting" all of the information they give us. Of course, in that case, the Germans were doing it on purpose—they weren't giving up the cipher—but Turing and the Enigma serve as a contrast for what we should do in our daily lives. Whenever we send a message, we should make it as *easy* to decrypt as possible.

What about decrypting other people's messages? Luckily, we can build our "ciphers" from skills and tools we use every day. We must employ empathy and situational awareness to communicate (and listen) in such a way that those who receive our message will have the least amount of ambiguity, make the fewest assumptions, and hopefully result in the least amount of miscommunication.

The Imitation Game allows us to make example of Turing in a couple of ways. In the movie, there is also a subplot about Turing's difficulties communicating with the general public. He had an extremely difficult time relating to people, even those with whom he worked on a daily basis who had intellects to rival his own. He understood words exactly as they would be defined in the dictionary, without interpreting the context and tone as part of the true meaning of others' messages. As such, he couldn't detect sarcasm, nor could he understand jokes or non-verbal cues. Turing considered interpersonal conversation a kind of cryptography because he rarely possessed the decryption skills to understand exactly what another person was saying and, more importantly, what they were implying.

Turing's own weakness in detecting social cues is a good parallel for electronic communications in the workplace today. Think of how often people's tones of voice or physical cues indicate their intended sarcasm or joviality in an everyday conversation. However, not all modes of communication leave room for those cues. Since most communication now happens electronically, we must update our end-based communication ciphers to factor in the mode of communication we're using. The toneless, expressionless, equivocal nature of electronic communication means that we have to work harder to be fully clear in our communications.

Ends-based communication is the most effective way of exchanging information. As demonstrated in *The Imitation Game*, effectiveness in communication can change the fates of the biggest undertakings, including a world war. Turing's team prevented an estimated 14 million to 21 million other people from dying just by figuring out how to decrypt messages. That skill could probably help any of us.

Of course, you won't kill 14 million people by sending a poorly-worded email, but no one wants to make a mistake; no one wants to hurt you or anyone else. Businesses, in various ways, lose potential profits and waste resources every day—but, over time, how many days, weeks, or months of work have been lost because of misinterpreted correspondence? Too many. In an effort to turn the tide, we have provided you with the tools you need to build your own "personal cipher" in five easy steps:

1. **Who is hearing the message?** Know your audience. Are you talking to a client, an employee, or your superior? Also, take into account your previous correspondence with that person. Some people prefer more formal business writing with all of the technical jargon included so they have details; others prefer a high-level overview to get their bearings before jumping into the weeds. Knowing which way the receiver prefers to communicate expedites the information processing and deliverables.

2. **What are they hearing?** Think about the content. Is this good news they will be excited about, or are you delivering something they won't want to hear? The content being delivered dictates the context in which to set the information.

3. **When are they hearing it?** The first email of the day is read differently than the last. On the same note, a message on Monday morning will be processed differently than a message on a Thursday afternoon before a holiday weekend. Should this be the case? No, but humans are not machines. Being conscious of when the communication is taking place can improve response.

4. **Why are they hearing it?** The person listening has to allocate already-tight resources to another project because of this communication. The budget is expanding and you need his or her proposal on why he or she should receive some of the excess funding. What do you want the other person's reaction to be? Let your desired outcome inform the context of the content.

5. **How do you expect them to react?** If you can anticipate the follow-up questions or reactions, you will be better prepared to further clarify the message.

We live our lives in a cryptographical world of back story, intonation, colloqui-alisms, unique references, job-specific jargon, and all other kinds of codes. Our job as communicators is to decrypt our message for our receivers so that they get the point of what we're really trying to say. Being explicit, empathetic, and clear, as well as checking them for understanding, are our best keys to making sure that we haven't overly encrypted a message that, when misinterpreted, will cause confusion, delays, and heartache. Ends-based communication is the only way to communicate efficiently and effectively.

CHAPTER 23

Reading People with *The Simpsons'* Australian Toilet Premise

by Joe DeSensi and Susan Draus

Everyone who's been through a management class knows that the standard responsibilities of a leader are planning, organizing, controlling, and motivating employees. Remember, before you start, that the last of those is the most important; it does not matter how well you plan, organize, or control if your employees are not motivated to perform at their best abilities and achieve consistent high results. To have a work force that is motivated, you must understand their hearts and minds and find the motivation techniques that will work on the greatest percentage of your work force.

Reason helps the employee's ability to understand how they are performing a specific task, but motivation is an employee's willingness to work at a certain level of effort. You can logic or brow-beat employees into a mode of compliance, but to truly motivate them, you must first understand their perceptions of the work place, the work force, and the work itself to confirm that you, as a leader, are sharing the same reality with the employee. If your spheres of perception do not coincide, you essentially inhabit different versions of reality and have a slim-to-none chance of achieving the desired outcome. If this is the case, it is difficult to plan strategically for creating a highly engaged workforce. We have conducted hundreds of leadership and employee interviews and focus groups. When it comes to how people feel, we learn more in the opening facial tics, scrunched brows, eye rolling, wide-eyed enthusiasm, and deflated posture than we do in the ensuing sentences of "content" they will give when answering a question. We call this the Simpson Australian Toilet Premise.

This bears a bit of explanation. In an episode of the cartoon series *The Simpsons*, the Simpson family travels to Australia. When they visit the US embassy, the toilet has a huge contraption connected to it. The ambassador explains that, since Australia is in the Southern Hemisphere, the flushing water naturally spins in the opposite direction as it does in America (which is in the Northern Hemisphere). A few seconds into the flushing process, the contraption attached to the toilet forces the water in the bowl to switch directions and spin the other way as it flushes—opposite the way an Australian toilet would normally flush. The Australians installed this contraption because they think that Americans will feel more at home if the toilets flush in the same direction as in America.

Oddly specific though the reference, you'll see a similar thing happen in interviews. You ask a question. There is an initial, unguarded reaction. Then, the "spin machine" kicks in and they start going in another direction. In some cases, people spin their answers because they don't feel comfortable sharing direct and honest feedback for fear of the reaction from the room. In other cases, they have an agenda they want to push and will spin-doctor their way to the subject, no matter what question is asked. Still other times, their brain really wants them to feel a certain way about something even if their heart isn't in it (in these cases, they're spinning themselves more than anyone else).

This last version of spinning is not any more difficult to mitigate than the others, but you must decipher where his or her true interests lay. To that end, ask how someone feels about something; in the first few seconds of their answer, you'll receive the most useful data to move forward with. The initial flash of interest, disgust, frustration, or excitement gives you a starting point to strategically present the rest of the information. As far as doing "understanding checks," policy and procedure alignment and congruency, brainstorming, and other data gathering exercises, you might use more of a Socratic process to unearth the content you need.

Specifically in regard to feelings, you'll find the most information *before* the spin machine kicks in. Other than during the interview process, there are several opportunities to gather this first-look kind of information. For instance, when one person is talking about something that sounds like a major initiative or issue, try to watch the reactions of others in the group. Consider taking down notes; capture as much helpful detail or nuance as you can, since you won't recall the meeting so well at a later date. When I do this, my notes ensure that I don't lose important points, they allow me to break eye contact without looking like I'm not paying attention, and finally, they allow me to scan the group for what is not being said. This is not to say that what is being said isn't important—but it's important because you get to see the thinking or information processing of the person talking, which in many cases is the most important data collection of an interview, more important than the answers themselves. It's this data that helps you determine how an idea is being received.

Take, for example, the end of a good quarter. Factually, the company or department in question might have had their best quarter ever. As people who are concerned with more than the bottom line itself, we need to remember that our measures do not stop there. From an employees' perspective, they may have worked many nights and weekends to achieve this end goal and they might feel as though they've been taken for granted—or at least need some appreciation for their sacrifices. Disgruntled workers do not perform to their full capabilities, and as a result it may get harder to reach those same numbers again—either because they are not performing at optimum capacity (because they are no longer motivated) or because turnover has increased as a result of lack of appreciation.

We should not be surprised by others' reactions if we ask, but instead, we should use it as an opportunity to ask why and improve upon our understanding of the situation. If you know the true landscape of the work place and have a finger on the pulse of the work force, you become a more effective leader. Consider your audience and create opportunities to observe initial behaviors to craft a strategy to increase interest and effectiveness.

Feelings are challenging to read and even tougher to address (much less change). Many people are uncomfortable with direct questions or feedback, but the answers are essential data points in developing effective motivational strategies. In those few precious moments before the mind starts to reshape or confuse those visceral gut reactions, you might not be given enough information to act upon, but maybe you'll hear enough to identify where to probe further. (Remember that answers to these questions are data points, not decision points.)

To get beyond satisfying and to start motivating and to create a workplace that provides the opportunity for self-actualization, you must be able to identify what drives your people and how they think. Incorporating their feelings into your strategic planning model and sharing common, empathetic understanding of initiatives and events is one of the best ways to motivate and retain your best employees. Find a motivation technique that engages your workforce and your retention will increase. In this way, you not only create value-add for your company, but also lose costs associated with having to recruit and train new hires.

CHAPTER 24

A Lesson in Assuming from *The Usual Suspects*

by Joe DeSensi and Susan Draus

The Usual Suspects is one of the best whodunits ever made. The cast of characters is incredible, the mystery is top-notch, and it has one of the best closing scenes (and closing lines) of any movie ever made. If you haven't seen this movie, stop reading and go watch it. **Spoiler alert: continuing to read this chapter will ruin the movie for anyone who has not seen it. If you don't care, keep reading.**

Throughout the course of the movie, the crippled and bumbling Verbal Kint, one of the "usual suspects" in a band of thieves, tells the police about the series of events that led to a bloody massacre and explosion at the docks. Over the course of an afternoon in the police station, Verbal delves into the tale, telling them about the other "usual suspects" and giving his insights on who could not be the perpetrator for whom the police are looking, his story remaining within the lead officer's operating assumptions. The police are satisfied by Verbal's story and allow him to leave on bail, believing they have been able to learn more about what happened from him. The police are confident that they have put in order what has happened, and that the suspected criminal responsible, a terrifying mobster named Keyser Söze, died in the explosion.

At the end of the movie, the agent realizes that Verbal's entire story was made up. From his chair in the agent's office, Verbal had masterfully woven together the names from random objects in the office (such as "Redfoot" and

"Kobayashi") into a sensible story. The agent was supremely confident that he knew what had happened, that he knew who the players were, and "Verbal" made his story play into it. The agent never realized that Keyser Söze was, in fact, sitting in front of him the whole time. And just like that—poof—*he's gone.* The agent's opportunity of a lifetime vanished before his eyes.

The hubris and confidence of the agent led him away from properly understanding his own story as it was happening. There are some things that we can learn from the way Keyser Söze, as Verbal, was able to escape capture:

1. **Never assume you have 100% of the information.** We are all susceptible to confirmation bias when we only hear and remember the things we want to be told. Other times, if something seems complete, we stop digging for new information. Rarely do we ever get all of the information, so if we feel like we have it all, we are probably making some assumptions or filling in some blanks ourselves. It's true that we don't need all of the information to make decisions, but we tend to make bolder moves when we are supremely confident, and this can sometimes be hazardous.

2. **Corroborate important information through independent sources.** On big-ticket decisions, one source of information is rarely enough. If there is information on which much of the decision-making is founded, then the information should be vetted through a few different sources. Most of us get our news or our gossip from single sources. Sources can be wrong, can lie, can be jaded by their own perspective, or can be incomplete. The bigger the decision, the more important it us for us to vet our information. Moreover, see the sources for what they are; don't take a single source as an authority, but rather, search for the strengths and weaknesses of the source that may be influence its information.

3. **Never assume you are the smartest person in the room.** If we overestimate our intellect in comparison to those around us, it usually makes us lazier; we don't prepare as well or argue our points as well. We need to assume that the people with whom we are talking are sharks and

know more than we do (especially if we are negotiating). It is better to be over-prepared even at the expense of extra time than to find out you brought a knife to a gunfight. Another good thing about overestimating people is that you rarely come off as condescending or unengaged; if we think we are equally matched or maybe even bested, we are more likely to bring our A-game naturally.

4. **You never know exactly what someone's agenda will be.** Even if you think you have a pretty good idea, keep an open mind. One of the most common mistakes that I see in business discussions and negotiations is imputing (or assuming) the wrong intent from another person. We often assume people have the same understanding of good and bad, right and wrong, and believe in the same paths to success. This is almost never the case. Many more arguments occur between people who lack a shared perception (who have different premises, if you will) than between people who draw different conclusions from some shared understanding. Also, do not assume that someone's arguments exactly match their true motivations or agenda; some people use spin to convince others in their favor. For example, a person might argue to kill a project, positioning it as an "unnecessary allocation of resources," when the real reason they don't want the project is because some of their people would be pulled for that project. Offering probing questions and alternative solutions specifically targeted at the issues that they present helps figure out if the issues someone states are the true problem—or if there is something else going on that the person isn't saying. If you are not addressing the root cause of something, you are not efficiently addressing the problem.

5. **Don't be too paranoid, even if you're rightfully critical.** Again on the issue of imputing intent, I see people sometimes go way down the rabbit hole and assume someone has evil intent, or that the person is "just trying to thwart something good." In my experience, incorrect assumptions usually stem from one of two things: (1) a lack of common reality about priorities or the reasons something is being done, or (2) differing measures of success, where different groups prioritize different metrics

and view success differently, but without being explicit and discussing their standards with one another. (Compounding the problem: not only do many groups not discuss their standards for success, but they have to guess what other people's standards are. This can become messy.) So if you are worried about budget, but they are worried about time, how each of you weight the key decisions in a project or initiative can be radically different.

One of the things that *The Usual Suspects* teaches us is to try not to fit everything into our predefined narrative, but rather, to critically self-reflect on the narrative we're creating to search for holes. This involves understanding others, looking for pieces that don't seem to fit, "trusting but verifying," remaining open to new information and re-evaluating what you believe you know. Don't get cocky and let your gut tell you that you have it all figured out—only to find out that you've missed the opportunity of a lifetime.

CHAPTER 25

Our Town:
Lessons for LEADing Your Life

by Hope Zoeller

Thornton Wilder's 1938 play *Our Town* recently came to, well, our town. While I had already known the play well, something about this performance struck me differently; perhaps it's getting older and reflecting more on life's experiences. As we age, each moment becomes more precious. The simple things become the things that make us happiest. We realize the battles that are worth fighting and the ones that are best surrendered. We make peace by letting go of things that do not serve us well.

Our Town is set in the fictional American small town of Grover's Corners. It tells the story of an average town's citizens in the early twentieth century as depicted through their everyday lives. It is broken into three acts: Daily Life, Love & Marriage, and Death & Dying. What you see played out in these acts is the struggle to appreciate the beauty of everyday life.

Below are lessons for "LEADing" your life from the characters and citizens of Grover's Corners:

LIVE in the moment. Be present wherever you are and in whatever you are doing; it makes for a richer and more meaningful experience. Next time you feel yourself drifting from the present, try to bring yourself back to wherever you are. Realize that this moment is precious and never to be lived again, so be in it. As Horace the poet said in 23 BC, *carpe diem*—seize the day!

EMBRACE the beauty around you. Many of us are always rushing to get to the next meeting, the next project, the next day, even the next season. As soon as the snow falls, we wish it were spring. As soon as it is spring, we wish it were fall. Never are we truly appreciating the beauty of this moment of this season of our life. This results in missing many of life's sweetest moments. As Henry David Thoreau so eloquently said, "You must live in the present, launch yourself on every wave, find your eternity in each moment. Fools stand on their island of opportunities and look toward another land. There is no other land; there is no other life but this."

APPRECIATE the efforts of others. Celebrate their successes as if they were your own. According to researcher Tom Rath at Gallup, the number one reason why people quit their jobs is lack of appreciation. Everyone wants to feel significant, to be recognized for what they do. As nineteenth-century British Prime Minister Benjamin Disraeli said, "The greatest good you can do for another is not just to share your riches but to reveal to him his own."

DEDICATE your life to others. It's not about how much we get in life; it's about how much we give. If you truly desire happiness, seek and serve others. Share knowledge and resources. Make introductions. Recognize the accomplishments of others. Volunteer your time. In the words of Mahatma Gandhi, "The best way to find yourself is to lose yourself in the service of others." By helping others, you are leading yourself to success.

"Oh earth, you're too wonderful for anybody to realize you. Do any human beings ever realize life while they live it? Every, every minute?"

Here's to appreciating and living every, every minute!

Suggested Reading

10-10-10 (10 Minutes, 10 Months, 10 Years: A Life Transforming Idea) by Suzy Welch

The 15 Invaluable Laws of Growth by John C. Maxwell

The Art of War for Women by Chin-Ning Chu

Brothers, Rivals, Victors by Jonathan W. Jordan

Change Anything—The New Science of Personal Success by Kerry Patterson

The Confidence Code by Katty Kay and Claire Shipman

Cracking the Corporate Code by Price M. Cobbs and Judith L. Turnock

Creating Women's Networks by Catalyst & Foreword by Sheila W. Wellington

Crucial Conversations by Kerry Patterson, Ron McMillan, Al Switzler, Joseph Grenny

Daring Greatly by Brene Brown

Developing the Leader Within You by John C. Maxwell

Drive by Daniel Pink

Don't Retire, Rewire! by Jeri Sedlar and Rick Miners

Do What You Love, The Money Will Follow by Marsha Sinetar

Failing Forward: Turning Mistakes into Stepping Stones for Success by John C. Maxwell

The First 90 Days by Michael Watkins

The Five Dysfunctions of a Team by Patrick Lencioni

The 4 Disciplines of Execution: Achieving Your Wildly Important Goals by Chris McChesney and Sean Covey

Good to Great by Jim Collins

Go Put Your Strengths to Work by Marcus Buckingham

Hiring Made Easy as PIE: The Hiring Manager's Guide to Selecting the Best-Fit Employee by Alonzo Johnson

The Integrity Dividend by Tony Simons

Leaders Open Doors, 2nd Edition: A Radically Simple Leadership Approach to Lift People, Profits, and Performance by Bill Treasurer

Leadership and The One Minute Manager by Ken Blanchard

Leadership Essentials for Women by Linda Clark

The Leadership Pipeline by Ram Charan and Stephen Drotter

Lean In: Women, Work, and the Will to Lead by Sheryl Sandberg

The Money is the Gravy: Finding the Career that Nourishes You by John Clark

The No Asshole Rule by Robert I. Sutton

On Your Mark: From First Word to First Draft in Six Weeks by Cathy Fyock and Kevin Williamson

Outliers: The Story of Success by Malcolm Gladwell

Performance by Bill Treasurer

Play Like a Man, Win Like a Woman by Gail Evans

The Power of Personal Accountability by Mark Samuel and Sophie Chiche

The Power of Resilience: Achieving Balance, Confidence, and Personal Strength in Your Life by Robert Brooks

Principle Centered Leadership by Stephen Covey

Quiet Leadership by David Rock

The Secrets of Savvy Networking: How to Make the Best Connections for Business and Personal Success by Susan Roane

Seven Habits of Highly Effective People by Stephen Covey

Seven Secrets of Successful Women by Donna Brooks and Lynn Brooks

Slowing Down to the Speed of Life: How to Create a More Peaceful Simpler Life from the Inside Out by Richard Carlson and Joseph Bailey

Start with Why: How Great Leaders Inspire Everyone to Action by Simon Sinek

The Spark, the Flame, and the Torch by Lance Secretan

The Speed of Trust by Stephen Covey

Team Based Strategic Planning by C. Davis Fogg

Trust & Betrayal in the Workplace: Building Effective Relationships in Your Organization by Dennis S. Reina, Ph.S. and Michelle L. Reina, Ph.D.

Turning Around Turnaround Schools: What to Do When Conventional Wisdom and Best Practice Aren't Enough by Frank DeSensi, Robert Knight, and Joe DeSensi

The Upside of Down: Why Failing Well is the Key to Success by Megan McArdle

What Color is Your Parachute? 2015: A Practical Manual for Job-Hunters and Career-Changers by Richard N. Bolles

What Got You Here Won't Get You There by Marshall Goldsmith with Mark Reiter

Who Says It's a Man's World? by Emily Bennington

Write to the Top: Writing for Corporate Success by Deborah Dumaine

The Woman's Advantage by Mary Cantando

A Little More About HOPE

Helping Other People Excel, LLC (HOPE) is a leadership development firm. We specialize in professional development for leaders at every level of the organization. For readers that might not be familiar with us, we wanted to share a little more information about ourselves.

We help companies perform better from the top down. We build leadership capacity, help corporate-wide communication, and help understand what motivates and inspires the real people at a company. We don't produce magic business bullets. We get in, do the hard work to figure out where a company is and where they want to go, and then we build a real path to get them there.

Many leadership consulting firms have a set plan or a core ideology around which their consulting must bend. We take the approach of *what are you doing, who are you*, and *what can make you better*. Real company change has to be context-based, meaning there isn't an ivory-tower solution. Different people and different cultures have different needs.

If you have a critical vocabulary based around a certain management philosophy, let's use it to build something new. If you have an idea of what your company needs, but you need someone to build a custom leadership program, we can do that. If you just want your people to have a couple hours a week to bounce ideas off experts in an informal setting, we can do it. Our ability to work inside of a business's framework allows us to deliver training and coaching that meet the specific needs of our clients.

We run the company with the same philosophy with which we help clients. We are all experts, and we are all learners. Different people take leadership positions based on need. We are a flat company, more of a cohort of piers than a hierarchical structure. We integrate fun into business and life. We have accumulated our consultants over 20 years in the industry; they are our friends as well as our partners. There is mutual trust and mutual admiration. We have a great time doing what we love doing.

For more information about our leadership development services, visit us at www.hopeforleaders.com or email us at info@hopeforleaders.com.